Published by
Rupa Publications India Pvt. Ltd 2025
7/16, Ansari Road, Daryaganj
New Delhi 110002

Sales centres:
Bengaluru Chennai
Hyderabad Jaipur Kathmandu
Kolkata Mumbai Prayagraj

Copyright © Rupa Publications India Pvt. Ltd 2025

The views and opinions expressed in this book are the
authors' own and the facts are as reported by him which
have been verified to the extent possible, and the publishers
are not in any way liable for the same.

All rights reserved.
No part of this publication may be reproduced, transmitted,
or stored in a retrieval system, in any form or by any means,
electronic, mechanical, photocopying, recording or otherwise,
without the prior permission of the publisher.

Photo Source: Wikimedia Commons

ISBN: 978-93-6156-914-2

First impression 2025

10 9 8 7 6 5 4 3 2 1

The moral right of the author has been asserted.

Printed in India

This book is sold subject to the condition that it shall not,
by way of trade or otherwise, be lent, resold, hired out, or otherwise
circulated, without the publisher's prior consent, in any form of
binding or cover other than that in which it is published.

CONTENTS

Introduction 5

1. The History of Boxing 9

SECTION ONE
GETTING STARTED

2. Understanding Boxing as a Sport 21
3. Equipment and Gear 33
4. Boxing Stance and Footwork 47

SECTION TWO:
LEARNING THE BASICS

5. Basic Punches and Combinations 65
6. Defensive Techniques 77
7. Sparring and Drills 91

SECTION THREE
CONDITIONING AND TRAINING

8. Physical Conditioning for Boxers — 103
9. Nutrition and Diet — 113

SECTION FOUR
ADVANCED TECHNIQUES AND STRATEGY

10. Advanced Punching Techniques — 121
11. Advanced Defensive Tactics — 130
12. Nurturing a Future Olympic Boxer — 139
13. Filipino Olympians in Boxing: A Legacy of Courage and Skill — 143

List of Olympic Medalists (2000–2024) — 148

INTRODUCTION

Boxing is a sport that transcends mere physical combat; it is an art form that requires discipline, strategy, and an unyielding spirit. From the moment a fighter steps into the ring, they are not just engaging in a contest of strength, but in a battle of wits and willpower. This book is designed to take you on a journey through the world of boxing, offering insights into its rich history, technical skills, physical conditioning, and the mental toughness required to excel in the sport.

At its core, boxing is about more than just throwing punches. It is a test of endurance, timing, and precision. Every movement in the ring—from the subtle shift of the feet to the snap of a jab—has a purpose. Boxing is often described as "the sweet science," a term that encapsulates the sport's combination of physicality and intellectual rigor. It is a sport that demands not only physical prowess but also strategic thinking, as fighters must constantly anticipate and react to their opponent's moves.

The Evolution of Boxing

Boxing has a storied history that dates back thousands of years. It was practiced in ancient civilizations such as Egypt, Greece, and Rome, where it was often brutal and deadly. The sport evolved over the centuries, with rules gradually being introduced to protect fighters and ensure fair competition. The modern sport of boxing as we know it began to take shape in the 18th century with the introduction of the London Prize Ring Rules and later the Queensberry Rules, which standardized the use of gloves and rounds.

As boxing gained popularity, it produced legendary fighters whose names are etched in history. Icons like Muhammad Ali, Mike Tyson, and Sugar Ray Leonard have become synonymous with the sport, their careers inspiring countless others to lace up their gloves and step into the ring. These fighters not only showcased the physical demands of boxing but also highlighted the importance of mental toughness, resilience, and determination.

Why Learn Boxing?

Whether you are an aspiring professional, an amateur enthusiast, or someone looking to get fit, learning boxing offers numerous benefits. Physically, boxing is one of the most effective ways to build strength, endurance, and agility. It is a full-body workout that engages every muscle group, improving cardiovascular health and burning calories at a high rate.

Beyond the physical benefits, boxing teaches valuable life skills. The discipline required to train, the courage to

face an opponent, and the ability to stay calm under pressure are qualities that extend beyond the ring. Boxing builds confidence, sharpens focus, and instills a sense of respect for oneself and others.

This book is structured to guide you through every aspect of boxing. Starting with the fundamentals, you will learn about the basic techniques, the importance of proper equipment, and the role of conditioning. As you progress, you will delve into advanced strategies, mental preparation, and the intricacies of competitive boxing. Whether you are a beginner or have some experience, this book will provide you with the knowledge and tools to improve your skills and deepen your understanding of the sport.

Boxing is a journey—one that challenges you physically and mentally. By the end of this book, you will not only know how to box but also appreciate the depth and richness of the sport. Welcome to the world of boxing, where every punch tells a story, and every fight is a testament to the human spirit.

1

THE HISTORY OF BOXING

Origins of Boxing

BOXING IS ONE OF THE OLDEST SPORTS KNOWN TO humanity, with roots that trace back thousands of years. The sport has evolved significantly over time, but its fundamental premise—two individuals facing off in a contest of strength, skill, and endurance—remains the same.

The earliest evidence of boxing dates back to ancient Sumer, around 3000 BC, where carvings depict people striking each other with fists. These early contests were likely held as forms of entertainment or ritual, with fighters using their bare hands to strike opponents. Boxing was also practiced in ancient Egypt, where wall paintings from around 1350 BC depict scenes of fistfights, sometimes with crowds of spectators watching. These early versions of boxing were likely brutal and dangerous, with few, if any, rules to protect the participants.

The sport became more formalized in ancient Greece, where it was known as "pygmachia," or "fist fighting." Boxing was included in the ancient Olympic Games in 688 BC, making it one of the oldest competitive sports in history. Greek boxers, known as "pugilists," would wrap their hands and forearms in leather straps called "himantes" to protect their fists and inflict more damage on their opponents. These straps were often hardened to enhance their effectiveness, turning the hands into deadly weapons. Unlike modern boxing, there were no rounds or time limits in Greek boxing—fights continued until one fighter was knocked out or conceded defeat.

Boxers, terracotta figurine from Apulia, Magna Graecia, 3rd century BC

The Romans adopted boxing from the Greeks, but their version of the sport was even more brutal. Roman boxers used a type of glove called the "cestus," which was

loaded with metal or spikes to maximize injury. Boxing matches in Rome often took place in arenas and were part of the gladiatorial games, where fighters could face serious injury or death. Despite its violence, boxing was popular in Rome for centuries before declining in popularity with the fall of the Roman Empire.

With the collapse of the Roman Empire, boxing as a formal sport disappeared for many centuries. However, informal fistfights continued to be a popular pastime in various cultures around the world. It wasn't until the 17th century that boxing began to reemerge as a recognized sport, particularly in England.

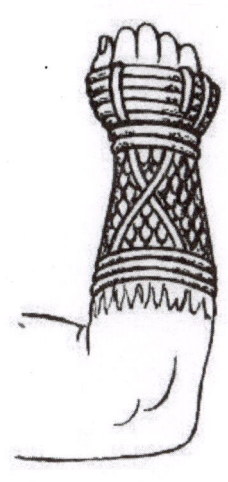

Cestus

Evolution of the Sport

The modern sport of boxing began to take shape in England during the 17th and 18th centuries. At this time, the sport was known as "prizefighting," and it was largely unregulated, with few rules governing how matches were conducted. Fights often took place in open fields or makeshift rings, and they attracted large crowds who would bet on the outcomes. The first major step towards modern boxing came in 1743 when Jack Broughton, a prominent English boxer, introduced the Broughton Rules. These rules were the first attempt to standardize boxing and make it safer for

participants. The Broughton Rules prohibited hitting a man while he was down and introduced a count of 30 seconds to allow a knocked-down fighter to recover. Despite these advancements, the sport was still rough and dangerous, with fighters often sustaining serious injuries.

Depiction of the 62-round prizefight at Banbury, England in 1789 between Tom Johnson (Champion of England) and Isaac Perrins

The sport continued to evolve over the next century, and in 1867, the Marquess of Queensberry introduced the Queensberry Rules, which laid the foundation for modern boxing. The Queensberry Rules mandated the use of gloves, which were padded to reduce the risk of injury, and introduced three-minute rounds with one-minute intervals between them. These rules also established weight classes to ensure fair competition, and they prohibited wrestling moves, emphasizing clean boxing techniques.

The introduction of the Queensberry Rules helped to legitimize boxing as a sport and contributed to its growing popularity. It was during this period that boxing began to

spread to other parts of the world, particularly the United States, where it quickly became a popular form of entertainment. The late 19th and early 20th centuries saw the rise of legendary fighters like John L. Sullivan, who became the first recognized heavyweight champion under the Queensberry Rules.

As boxing gained popularity, it also began to face scrutiny. Concerns about the safety of fighters and the sport's potential for corruption led to calls for greater regulation. In response, various

Portrait of the pugilist John 'Jack' Broughton

boxing commissions and governing bodies were established to oversee the sport and enforce rules designed to protect fighters. These organizations, such as the World Boxing Association (WBA), World Boxing Council (WBC), and International Boxing Federation (IBF), play a crucial role in maintaining the integrity of the sport and ensuring the safety of its participants.

Over the years, boxing has continued to evolve, with new techniques, training methods, and safety measures being introduced. Today, boxing is a global sport, with millions of fans and participants around the world. Despite the challenges it has faced, including concerns about the long-term health effects of repeated head trauma, boxing remains one of the most popular and respected combat sports in the world.

Famous Boxers and Iconic Matches

Throughout its history, boxing has produced some of the most legendary and celebrated athletes in the world of sports. These fighters have not only left their mark on the sport but have also become cultural icons, inspiring generations of fans and athletes.

One of the most famous boxers of all time is Muhammad Ali, who is widely regarded as one of the greatest athletes in history. Ali, born Cassius Clay, burst onto the scene in the 1960s with his incredible speed, agility, and charisma. He became the world heavyweight champion in 1964 when he defeated Sonny Liston in a major upset. Ali's career was marked by his rivalry with Joe Frazier, which produced some of the most iconic matches in boxing history, including the "Fight of the Century" in 1971 and the "Thrilla in Manila" in 1975. Ali's refusal to be drafted into the Vietnam War and his outspoken views on civil rights also made him a symbol of resistance and social justice, cementing his legacy both inside and outside the ring.

Image: Muhammad Ali

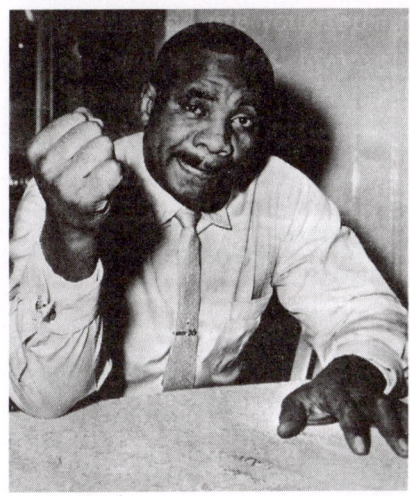

Sonny Liston

Another iconic figure in boxing history is Mike Tyson, who became the youngest heavyweight champion in history at the age of 20. Tyson was known for his ferocious power and aggressive style, which earned him the nickname "Iron Mike." During the late 1980s, Tyson dominated the heavyweight division, winning his first 37 professional fights and becoming one of the most feared fighters in the sport. Despite his later legal troubles and controversial behavior, Tyson remains one of the most recognizable and influential figures in boxing history.

Sugar Ray Leonard is another legendary boxer who made a significant impact on the sport. Leonard was known for his speed, skill, and versatility, and he became a five-weight world champion during his career. His fights against Thomas Hearns, Roberto Durán, and Marvin Hagler are considered some of the greatest bouts in boxing history. Leonard's

Joe Frazier

ability to adapt his style to different opponents and his charisma outside the ring made him a fan favorite and one of the most successful boxers of his era.

Floyd Mayweather Jr., who retired with an undefeated record of 50-0, is considered one of the greatest defensive boxers of all time. Known for his impeccable defense, lightning-fast reflexes, and ring intelligence, Mayweather dominated the sport for over two decades. His ability to neutralize his opponents' strengths and control the pace of fights earned him the nickname "Money," and he became one of the highest-paid athletes in the world. Despite criticism for his cautious fighting style, Mayweather's achievements in the ring are unparalleled, and he remains one of the most polarizing figures in boxing.

In addition to these iconic fighters, boxing has produced countless other legends, including Joe Louis, who reigned as heavyweight champion for over a decade; Rocky Marciano, who retired undefeated as the heavyweight champion; and Manny Pacquiao, who became the only boxer in history to win world titles in eight different weight classes. These fighters and their legendary matches have helped shape the history of boxing and have left a lasting legacy on the sport.

The Impact of Boxing on Society

Boxing has had a profound impact on society throughout its long history. The sport has not only produced legendary athletes but has also played a significant role in shaping cultural, social, and political movements.

Manny Pacquiao

One of the most notable impacts of boxing is its role as a pathway to success for individuals from disadvantaged backgrounds. Many of the greatest boxers in history, including Muhammad Ali, Mike Tyson, and Manny Pacquiao, came from humble beginnings. Boxing offered them a way to escape poverty and achieve fame and fortune. For many young people, especially in inner-city communities, boxing gyms provide a safe haven and a positive outlet for their energy, teaching discipline, respect, and perseverance.

Boxing has also been a platform for social change and activism. Muhammad Ali, for example, used his fame to speak out against racial injustice and the Vietnam War. His refusal to be drafted into the military, citing his opposition to the war on religious and ethical grounds, made him a controversial figure and a symbol of resistance during the civil rights movement. Ali's activism and his willingness to sacrifice his career for his beliefs had a lasting impact on American society and inspired other athletes to use their platforms to advocate for social change.

In addition to its role in social movements, boxing has also had a significant cultural impact. The sport has been the subject of countless films, books, and documentaries, many of which have become cultural touchstones. Movies like "Rocky," "Raging Bull," and "Million Dollar Baby" have not only depicted the drama and intensity of boxing but have also explored deeper themes of perseverance, redemption, and the human spirit. These films have helped to shape the public's perception of boxing and have contributed to the sport's enduring popularity.

Boxing has also played a role in bringing people together, transcending cultural and national boundaries. Major boxing events often draw huge audiences from around the world, uniting people in their love for the sport. The global nature of boxing has helped to foster cross-cultural exchange and understanding, as fighters from different countries and backgrounds compete on the world stage.

However, boxing has also faced criticism for the risks it poses to fighters. The long-term effects of repeated head trauma, including chronic traumatic encephalopathy (CTE), have raised concerns about the safety of the sport. While measures have been introduced to improve fighter safety, such as stricter medical protocols and the use of protective gear, the inherent risks of boxing continue to be a topic of debate.

Despite these challenges, boxing remains one of the most respected and celebrated sports in the world. Its rich history, cultural significance, and impact on society have made it an enduring and beloved sport, admired for its blend of athleticism, strategy, and sheer determination. Whether viewed as a pathway to success, a platform for social change, or a thrilling spectacle, boxing continues to captivate and inspire people around the globe.

SECTION ONE

GETTING STARTED

2

UNDERSTANDING BOXING AS A SPORT

What is Boxing?

BOXING IS A COMBAT SPORT WHERE TWO participants, known as boxers, face off against each other in a ring and aim to land punches on their opponent while avoiding being hit themselves. It's a sport that combines physical strength, endurance, speed, and strategic thinking. Unlike other combat sports, boxing is strictly about striking with the fists, making it a test of both power and precision.

The objective in boxing is simple: to outscore your opponent or to knock them out, rendering them unable to continue the fight. However, achieving this requires more than just brute force. Boxers must master a range of skills, including footwork, defensive maneuvers, and the ability to anticipate their opponent's moves. A well-rounded boxer is not only powerful but also quick, agile, and smart in the ring.

Boxing matches take place in a square ring, typically measuring 16 to 20 feet on each side, with ropes surrounding it. The fight is divided into rounds, usually three minutes each, with a one-minute rest between rounds. The number of rounds varies depending on the level of competition, ranging from four rounds for beginners to twelve rounds for championship bouts.

Boxing is often referred to as "the sweet science," a term that highlights the sport's blend of physical and mental challenges. Boxers must be in peak physical condition, but they also need to think strategically, setting traps for their opponent, countering attacks, and capitalizing on weaknesses. The sport requires a deep understanding of timing, distance, and angles, as well as the ability to remain calm and focused under pressure.

The Basic Rules and Regulations

Boxing is governed by a set of rules and regulations designed to ensure fair competition and the safety of the fighters. Understanding these rules is essential for anyone looking to get involved in the sport, whether as a competitor or as a fan.

1. **The Ring:** Boxing matches take place in a square ring, typically 16 to 20 feet on each side. The ring is surrounded by ropes, which provide a boundary for the fighters. Stepping outside the ropes is not allowed, and doing so can result in a warning or penalty.
2. **Rounds and Time:** A standard boxing match is divided into rounds, each lasting three minutes. There is a

one-minute rest period between rounds. The number of rounds varies based on the level of competition. Amateur bouts usually have three to four rounds, while professional bouts can have anywhere from four to twelve rounds. Championship fights are typically twelve rounds.

Boxing Ring

3. **Scoring:** In boxing, points are awarded based on clean punches, which are defined as punches that land with the knuckle part of the glove on the opponent's head or body. Judges also consider factors such as effective aggression, ring generalship (control of the fight), defense, and hard and clean punching. The 10-point must system is used in most professional boxing matches, where the winner of each round receives 10 points, and the loser receives 9 or fewer, depending on the round's performance.

4. **Knockdowns and Knockouts:** A knockdown occurs when a fighter is hit and any part of their body other than the feet touches the canvas, or when they are knocked through the ropes. The referee will issue a count of up to 10 seconds to determine if the fighter can continue. A knockout (KO) occurs when a fighter is unable to get up before the count of 10, resulting in an automatic victory for the opponent. A technical knockout (TKO) occurs when the referee, the fighter's corner, or the ringside doctor decides that the fighter cannot continue safely, even if they are still on their feet.

Knockdown

5. **Fouls and Penalties:** Certain actions are considered fouls in boxing and can result in warnings, point deductions, or disqualification. Common fouls include hitting below the belt, holding or wrestling, headbutting, hitting after the bell, and hitting an opponent who is down. The referee has the authority to enforce the rules and can penalize a fighter for repeated or severe fouls.
6. **Equipment:** Boxers are required to wear protective

equipment, including gloves, a mouthguard, and a groin protector. Gloves are padded to reduce the risk of injury and vary in weight depending on the boxer's weight class. The mouthguard protects the teeth and jaw, while the groin protector guards against low blows.

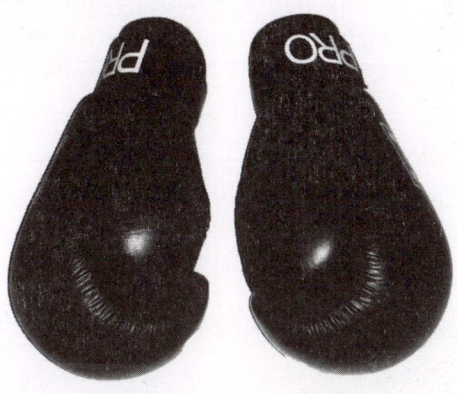

A pair of boxing gloves

Mouthguard

OLYMPIC SERIES: BOXING

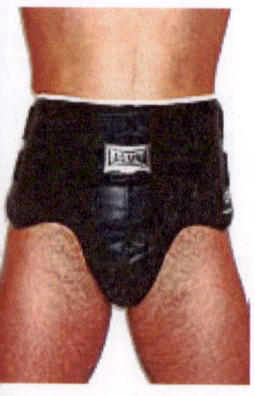

Groin Protector

7. **Referee's Role:** The referee is responsible for ensuring the safety of the fighters and enforcing the rules during the match. They can stop the fight if they believe a fighter is in danger, issue warnings or penalties for fouls, and make the final decision in case of a knockout or technical knockout.

Understanding these rules and regulations is crucial for both fighters and fans, as they ensure that boxing remains a fair and competitive sport.

Referee

The Role of Boxing Organizations (WBA, WBC, IBF, etc.)

Boxing is a global sport, and its professional ranks are overseen by several major organizations that govern the sport, sanction championship bouts, and set the standards for competition. The most prominent of these organizations are the World Boxing Association (WBA), the World Boxing Council (WBC), the International Boxing Federation (IBF), and the World Boxing Organization (WBO).

1. **World Boxing Association (WBA):** Established in 1921, the WBA is the oldest of the four major boxing organizations. Originally known as the National Boxing Association (NBA), it changed its name to the WBA in 1962 to reflect its growing international presence. The WBA is responsible for sanctioning championship fights and ranking fighters within its organization. It also sets rules and regulations for its title fights, including the number of rounds and the mandatory defenses that champions must make to retain their titles.

2. **World Boxing Council (WBC):** Founded in 1963, the WBC is one of the most prestigious boxing organizations in the world. The WBC has been instrumental in implementing safety measures in the sport, such as the introduction of the 12-round limit for championship fights (down from 15 rounds) and the use of medical pre-fight examinations. The WBC also maintains its own rankings and awards championship belts to fighters who win its sanctioned title fights.

3. **International Boxing Federation (IBF):** The IBF was established in 1983 and quickly became one of the leading organizations in professional boxing. The IBF is known for its strict enforcement of rules and regulations, particularly regarding drug testing and the mandatory defenses that champions must make. Like the WBA and WBC, the IBF ranks fighters in each weight class and sanctions championship bouts.
4. **World Boxing Organization (WBO):** The WBO was founded in 1988 and is the youngest of the four major boxing organizations. Despite its relatively recent establishment, the WBO has gained significant recognition and respect in the boxing world. The WBO follows similar procedures to the other major organizations, ranking fighters, sanctioning title fights, and awarding championship belts. Over the years, the WBO has grown in prominence, particularly in Europe and Latin America.

These organizations play a crucial role in maintaining the structure and integrity of professional boxing. They provide a framework for competition, ensuring that fighters are matched fairly and that titles are contested according to a consistent set of rules. Each organization also has its own championship belts, and it is not uncommon for a fighter to hold titles from multiple organizations simultaneously, a feat known as "unification."

While the presence of multiple organizations can sometimes lead to confusion or disputes over rankings and title legitimacy, these bodies are essential in regulating the sport and ensuring that boxing remains competitive and

fair. They also help to promote the sport globally, organizing events and working to grow the fan base.

Weight Classes and Their Importance

Weight classes are a fundamental aspect of boxing, designed to ensure fair competition by matching fighters of similar size and weight. This system is crucial because, in a sport where physical strength and endurance are key, even a small weight difference can provide a significant advantage.

Boxing weight classes range from the smallest, like the **Minimum weight** (105 pounds or 47.6 kg), to the largest, **Heavyweight** (over 200 pounds or 90.7 kg). Each weight class has its own set of champions, and fighters typically compete within their designated class based on their natural body weight and their ability to make weight before a fight.

1. **Minimum weight/Straw weight** (up to 105 lbs/47.6 kg): The lightest class in professional boxing, where fighters are known for their speed and agility. Fights in this class are often fast-paced, with boxers relying on quick combinations and sharp footwork.
2. **Light Flyweight** (108 lbs/49.0 kg): A slightly heavier class than Minimum weight, featuring fighters who still emphasize speed but with a bit more power behind their punches.
3. **Flyweight** (112 lbs/50.8 kg): Known for quick and nimble fighters, this class has produced many exciting bouts, with boxers displaying both speed and technical skills.

4. **Super Flyweight** (115 lbs/52.2 kg): A weight class where fighters begin to showcase a blend of speed, power, and stamina, often leading to highly competitive matches.
5. **Bantamweight** (118 lbs/53.5 kg): Fighters in this class are known for their balance of speed and punching power, making for dynamic and entertaining fights.
6. **Super Bantamweight** (122 lbs/55.3 kg): A weight class where fighters often exhibit a mix of speed and increasing power, leading to thrilling exchanges in the ring.
7. **Featherweight** (126 lbs/57.2 kg): This class has a rich history of producing legendary fighters. Boxers here are known for their all-around abilities, combining speed, technique, and power.
8. **Super Featherweight** (130 lbs/59.0 kg): Also known as Junior Lightweight, this class often features fighters who are slightly heavier but still maintain the quickness associated with lighter divisions.
9. **Lightweight** (135 lbs/61.2 kg): A very competitive class where fighters combine speed, skill, and growing power. Many iconic bouts have taken place in this division.
10. **Super Lightweight** (140 lbs/63.5 kg): Also known as Junior Welterweight, fighters in this class begin to showcase significant power along with their technical skills.
11. **Welterweight** (147 lbs/66.7 kg): One of the most popular and competitive weight classes in boxing history, known for its mix of speed, power, and technical prowess. Some of the greatest boxers have competed in this division.

UNDERSTANDING BOXING AS A SPORT

12. **Super Welterweight** (154 lbs/69.9 kg): Also known as Junior Middleweight, this class often features hard-hitting fighters with a combination of speed and power.
13. **Middleweight** (160 lbs/72.6 kg): A historic and highly respected division where fighters are known for their power and endurance. Middleweight champions often gain significant recognition in the sport.
14. **Super Middleweight** (168 lbs/76.2 kg): A relatively recent addition to boxing, this class is known for producing powerful fighters with the stamina to go the distance.
15. **Light Heavyweight** (175 lbs/79.4 kg): This division features fighters with a potent mix of speed and significant punching power. The class has seen some of the most memorable bouts in boxing history.
16. **Cruiserweight** (200 lbs/90.7 kg): The division between Light Heavyweight and Heavyweight, known for fighters who have the power of heavyweights but often retain more speed and mobility.
17. **Heavyweight** (over 200 lbs/90.7 kg): The highest weight class, known for producing some of the most famous boxers in history. Heavyweights are known for their knockout power and often bring significant public attention to the sport.

The importance of weight classes cannot be overstated. They ensure that fighters compete on a level playing field, where skill, strategy, and conditioning are the deciding factors rather than sheer size. Fighters often have to undergo rigorous training and diet regimens to make weight before

a fight, which adds another layer of discipline and strategy to the sport.

For a fighter, choosing the right weight class is crucial. Some boxers may "move up" or "move down" in weight classes to find the division where they are most comfortable and competitive. Moving up in weight usually means facing bigger and stronger opponents, while moving down can provide a speed advantage but requires strict weight management.

Weight classes also add to the excitement of boxing, as they create opportunities for fighters to challenge themselves by competing in different divisions, leading to "super fights" between champions of different classes. This structure helps maintain the competitive balance of the sport and ensures that every fighter, regardless of size, has the opportunity to compete at the highest levels.

3

EQUIPMENT AND GEAR

Essential Boxing Gear: Gloves, Hand Wraps, Mouthguards, and More

BOXING IS A SPORT THAT REQUIRES A SIGNIFICANT amount of specialized equipment to ensure both the safety of the participants and the effectiveness of their training and competition. The right gear can make a substantial difference in performance and protection. This chapter provides a comprehensive guide to essential boxing gear, including gloves, hand wraps, mouthguards, and more, along with tips on choosing, maintaining, and caring for your equipment.

1. Boxing Gloves

Purpose and Importance: Boxing gloves are perhaps the most crucial piece of equipment in the sport. They are designed to protect both the boxer's hands and their opponent. The primary function of gloves is to cushion the impact of punches, which helps prevent injuries to the hands and reduces the risk of cuts and bruises to the opponent.

Types of Boxing Gloves:

- **Training Gloves**: These gloves are typically heavier and more padded, making them suitable for sparring and heavy bag workouts. They provide additional protection and are generally available in weights ranging from 12 to 16 ounces. Training gloves are designed to withstand the rigors of repeated punching and offer greater cushioning to protect the hands and wrists during intense practice sessions.

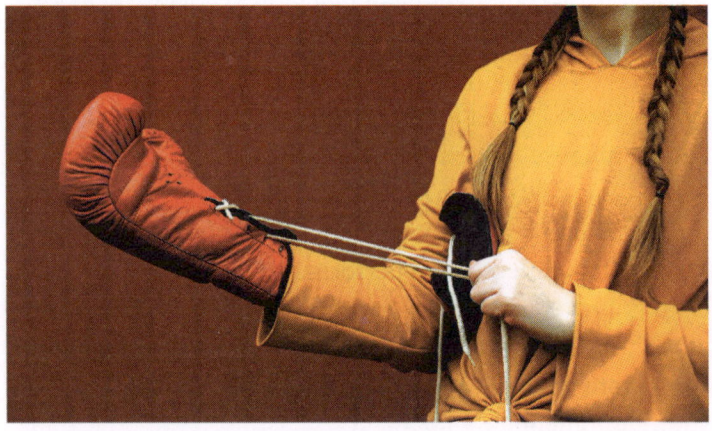

Training Gloves

- **Fight Gloves**: Also known as competition gloves, these are lighter and less padded compared to training gloves. They usually weigh between 8 to 10 ounces. The reduced padding allows for faster hand speed and greater impact

EQUIPMENT AND GEAR

during fights. Fight gloves are designed to deliver powerful punches while still offering a degree of protection.

- **Bag Gloves**: Designed specifically for use with heavy bags, these gloves offer less padding than training gloves. They help develop power and technique but are not suitable for sparring or competition.

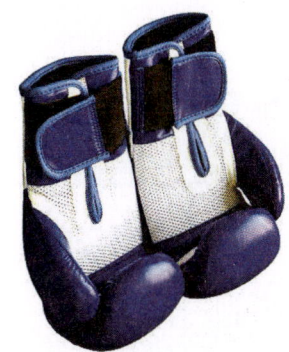

Fight Gloves

Bag gloves are usually lighter and focus on reinforcing the hands and wrists for striking heavy objects.

Choosing the Right Gloves: When selecting boxing gloves, consider the following factors:

- **Size and Fit**: Gloves should fit snugly but comfortably. Ensure there is enough room for hand wraps, and the glove should cover the knuckles adequately. A proper fit helps prevent injuries and ensures optimal performance.

Bag Gloves

- **Padding**: Choose gloves with appropriate padding for your needs. More padding is necessary for training and sparring, while lighter padding is suitable for competition.
- **Brand and Quality**: Invest in high-quality gloves from reputable brands to ensure durability and protection. Try on different brands to find the best fit and comfort.

2. Hand Wraps

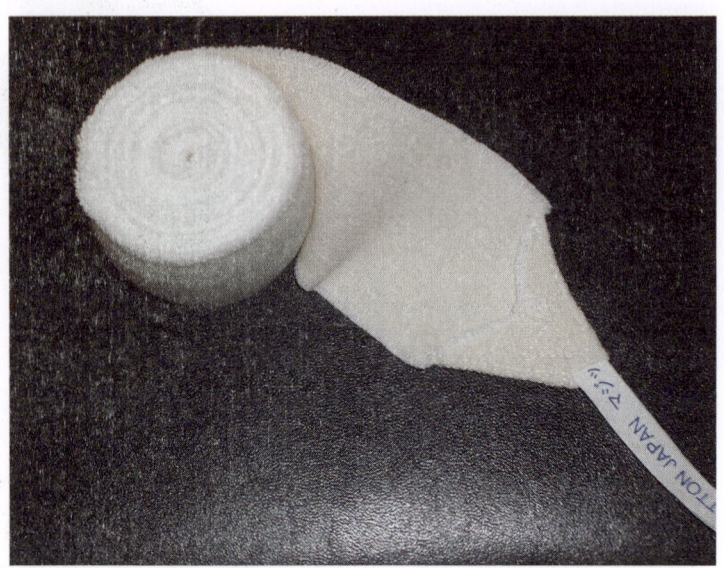

Bandage for amateur boxing in Japan

Purpose and Importance: Hand wraps are essential for protecting the bones and tendons in the hands and wrists. They provide support to the wrist joint and add padding over the knuckles, which helps prevent injuries during training and competition.

Types of Hand Wraps:

- **Traditional Wraps**: Made from cotton or elastic material, traditional hand wraps are wrapped around the hands and wrists to offer protection and support. They

are adjustable and can be customized to fit different hand sizes and preferences.

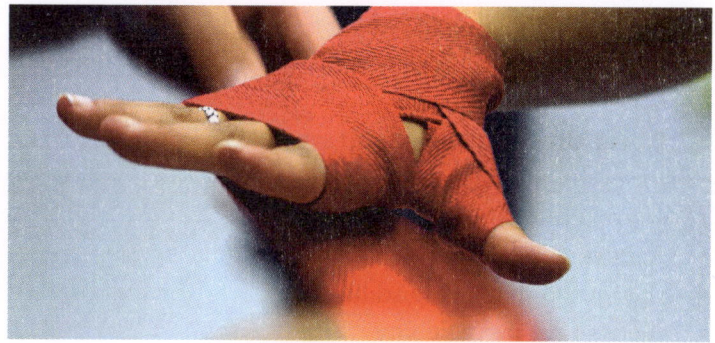

Traditional Wraps

- **Quick Wraps**: These are pre-formed wraps with built-in padding. Quick wraps are easy to use and can be slipped on quickly, making them a convenient option for those who need to wrap their hands quickly.

Quick Wraps

Applying Hand Wraps: Proper application of hand wraps is crucial for maximizing protection:

- **Start with the Wrist:** Begin wrapping from the base of the wrist and move towards the knuckles. This helps stabilize the wrist joint.
- **Cover the Knuckles:** Wrap around the knuckles several times to provide cushioning and support. Ensure the wraps are snug but not too tight.
- **Secure the Thumb:** If using traditional wraps, secure the thumb to provide additional protection and prevent the wraps from slipping.
- **Finish at the Wrist:** Complete the wrapping by securing the end around the wrist. Ensure the wraps are secure and comfortable, allowing for flexibility and movement.

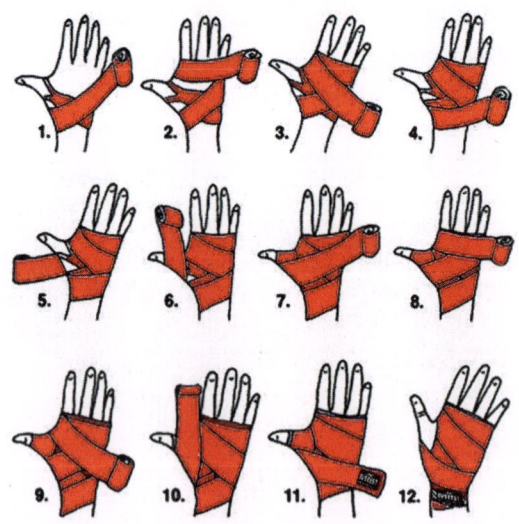

Steps to tie hand wraps

Choosing Hand Wraps:

- **Length:** Standard hand wraps are typically 180 inches long, providing sufficient coverage for most fighters. Shorter wraps (120 inches) are suitable for those with smaller hands.
- **Material:** Hand wraps come in cotton, elastic, or blended materials. Choose based on personal preference for comfort and flexibility.

3. Mouthguards

Purpose and Importance: Mouthguards are designed to protect the teeth, gums, and jaw from impact during boxing. They also help absorb some of the shock from punches, reducing the risk of concussions and jaw injuries.

Types of Mouthguards:

- **Boil-and-Bite:** Made from thermoplastic material, these mouthguards soften when heated and can be molded to fit the shape of your teeth. They offer a good balance of protection and comfort and are often more affordable than custom-fit options.
- **Custom-Fit:** Professionally made from molds of your teeth, custom-fit mouthguards provide the best protection and comfort. They are tailored to fit perfectly and offer superior coverage compared to boil-and-bite mouthguards.

Choosing a Mouthguard:

- **Fit and Comfort:** A well-fitting mouthguard should be comfortable and not obstruct breathing or speaking. It should cover all your teeth and fit snugly over the gums.
- **Material and Design:** Choose a mouthguard made from high-quality materials that offer durability and protection. Consider options with additional features like shock-absorption layers or extra cushioning.

4. Headgear

Purpose and Importance: Headgear protects the head, face, and ears from cuts, bruises, and impact injuries during sparring sessions. It also helps reduce the risk of concussions by absorbing some of the shock from punches.

Types of Headgear:

- **Training Headgear:** Provides more extensive padding around the forehead, cheeks, and chin. It is designed for use during sparring and offers maximum protection to prevent injuries.
- **Competition Headgear:** Lighter and less padded compared to training headgear, competition headgear is used in amateur boxing matches. It provides essential protection while allowing for greater visibility and mobility.

Training Headgear

Choosing Headgear:

- **Fit and Adjustability:** Headgear should fit snugly and comfortably, with adjustable straps to ensure a secure fit. It should cover the ears, forehead, and cheeks while allowing for clear vision.
- **Padding and Protection:** Select headgear with adequate padding to provide protection without compromising comfort or mobility.

Competition Headgear

5. Boxing Shoes

Purpose and Importance: Boxing shoes are designed to provide traction, support, and stability in the ring. They help boxers move quickly, maintain balance, and change direction with ease.

Types of Boxing Shoes:

- **High-Top Shoes:** Offer additional ankle support and are often preferred by boxers who need extra stability. They help prevent ankle injuries and provide greater support during movement.
- **Low-Top Shoes:** Provide greater freedom of movement and are favored by those who prioritize agility and quick footwork. They

High-top Boxing Shoes

are lighter and offer less ankle support but allow for faster movements.

Choosing Boxing Shoes:

- **Fit and Comfort:** Boxing shoes should fit snugly but not restrict movement. Ensure they provide adequate support for the ankles and allow for quick, agile movements.
- **Traction and Durability:** Look for shoes with good grip and traction to prevent slipping in the ring. They should also be durable and withstand the wear and tear of training.

6. Protective Cup

Purpose and Importance: A protective cup is worn by male fighters to safeguard the groin area from accidental blows. It is an essential piece of equipment for preventing injuries to this sensitive area.

Types of Protective Cups:

- **Hard Cups:** Made from rigid materials, hard cups offer strong protection and are typically worn with a jockstrap or compression shorts. They provide excellent coverage and durability.
- **Soft Cups:** More flexible and comfortable, soft cups offer moderate protection and are often used for training. They are designed to provide protection while allowing for greater mobility.

Choosing a Protective Cup:

- **Fit and Comfort:** The protective cup should fit securely and comfortably without restricting movement. Ensure it provides adequate coverage and protection for the groin area.

Choosing the Right Gear for You

Selecting the right boxing gear is essential for both performance and safety. Here are some tips for choosing the best equipment:

1. **Gloves:**
    - **Purpose:** Determine the primary use of the gloves (training, sparring, or competition) to select the appropriate type and weight.
    - **Fit:** Try on different gloves to find the best fit. Ensure they are comfortable, provide adequate wrist support, and fit snugly over hand wraps.
    - **Brand and Quality:** Invest in high-quality gloves from reputable brands. Look for gloves that offer durability and protection and read reviews or seek recommendations from experienced boxers.
2. **Hand Wraps:**
    - **Length and Material:** Choose hand wraps based on your hand size and preference for material. Longer wraps provide more coverage and support, while shorter wraps are suitable for those with smaller hands.
    - **Comfort:** Ensure the hand wraps are comfortable

and easy to apply. They should provide a secure fit without being too tight.

3. **Mouthguards:**
   - **Fit and Comfort:** Opt for a custom-fit mouthguard if possible for the best protection and comfort. Ensure it does not interfere with breathing or speaking.
   - **Material and Design:** Choose a mouthguard made from high-quality materials that offer durability and shock absorption.

4. **Headgear:**
   - **Fit and Protection:** Select headgear that fits snugly and provides adequate padding without obstructing vision. Adjustable straps help ensure a secure fit.
   - **Type:** Choose training headgear for sparring and competition headgear for matches, based on your needs.

5. **Boxing Shoes:**
   - **Fit and Comfort:** Boxing shoes should fit well and provide support for the ankles. They should be comfortable for extended wear and allow for quick movements.
   - **Traction and Durability:** Look for shoes with good grip and durability to ensure they perform well during training and competition.

6. **Protective Cup:**
   - **Fit and Comfort:** Ensure the protective cup fits securely and comfortably. It should provide adequate protection while allowing for unrestricted movement.

Maintaining and Caring for Your Equipment

Proper maintenance and care of boxing gear are essential for prolonging its lifespan and ensuring optimal performance. Here are some tips for keeping your equipment in top condition:

1. **Cleaning Gloves:**
   - **Air Dry:** After each use, allow gloves to air out to prevent moisture buildup and odor. Avoid exposing them to direct heat sources such as radiators or hair dryers.
   - **Antibacterial Spray:** Use a glove spray or powder designed for boxing gloves to reduce odor and bacteria. Follow the manufacturer's instructions for application.
   - **Cleaning the Liner:** If your gloves have removable liners, clean them regularly according to the manufacturer's instructions. Hand wash or use a gentle cycle in a laundry bag.
2. **Hand Wraps:**
   - **Washing:** Wash hand wraps after each use to remove sweat and bacteria. Hand wash them with mild detergent or use a gentle cycle in a laundry bag.
   - **Air Dry:** Allow hand wraps to air dry completely before storing them. Avoid using a dryer, as heat can damage the fabric.
3. **Mouthguards:**
   - **Rinsing:** Rinse the mouthguard with cold water after each use to remove debris and bacteria. Avoid using hot water, which can distort the shape.

- **Cleaning:** Clean the mouthguard weekly with mild soap and water. Use a soft brush to remove any buildup. Store it in a ventilated case to keep it clean and dry.
4. **Headgear:**
    - **Wiping Down:** After each use, wipe the headgear with a damp cloth to remove sweat and dirt. Avoid using harsh chemicals or abrasives.
    - **Air Dry:** Allow headgear to air dry fully before storing it to prevent odor and bacteria growth.
5. **Boxing Shoes:**
    - **Cleaning:** Wipe down boxing shoes with a damp cloth to remove dirt and sweat. Avoid submerging them in water, as this can damage the material.
    - **Air Out:** After each use, remove the insoles and let the shoes air out to prevent odor and moisture buildup.
6. **Protective Cup:**
    - **Rinsing and Drying:** Rinse the cup with water after each use and let it air dry before storing it. Check for any signs of wear or damage and replace it if necessary.

Proper care and maintenance of your boxing gear not only ensure its longevity but also contribute to your safety and performance. By investing in high-quality equipment and following these care tips, you'll be well-prepared for both training and competition.

4

BOXING STANCE AND FOOTWORK

BOXING IS NOT JUST ABOUT THROWING PUNCHES; it's a sophisticated sport where strategy, technique, and movement play pivotal roles. Central to these elements are the boxing stance and footwork, which form the bedrock of a boxer's performance. This chapter delves into the intricacies of boxing stance and footwork, breaking down their importance, exploring various stances, and providing a comprehensive guide to footwork fundamentals and drills to enhance these critical aspects of boxing.

The Importance of a Solid Stance

A boxer's stance is fundamental to their effectiveness in the ring. It impacts balance, power, defense, and overall movement. Here's an in-depth look at why a solid stance is crucial:

- **Balance and Stability:** A proper stance ensures that a boxer remains balanced and stable, even during the most dynamic movements. Without a solid stance, a boxer risks falling off balance, which can leave them vulnerable to counter-attacks. Balance is achieved through proper weight distribution between both feet and maintaining a low center of gravity. This stability allows a boxer to absorb and deflect incoming punches effectively.

- **Power Generation:** Power in boxing comes not just from the arm but from the whole body. A well-structured stance enables efficient weight transfer from the legs to the upper body, amplifying the force behind each punch. By anchoring the feet firmly on the ground, a boxer can utilize their body weight to deliver powerful blows, making each punch more effective and impactful.
- **Defense and Evasion:** A solid stance aids in defensive maneuvers. With the right stance, a boxer can shift weight quickly to evade punches and respond to attacks. This defensive capability is crucial for maintaining safety and exploiting openings in an opponent's defense. Proper stance allows for effective lateral movement, helping a boxer dodge punches and reposition strategically.
- **Mobility and Agility:** Footwork and mobility are critical for controlling the ring and executing strategies. A strong stance supports quick, agile movements and enables a boxer to maneuver around their opponent effectively. It facilitates smooth transitions between offensive and defensive positions and helps in maintaining proper distance from the opponent.

Basic Stances: Orthodox vs. Southpaw

Boxers typically adopt one of two primary stances: orthodox or southpaw. Understanding these stances is essential for both offensive and defensive strategies:

1. **Orthodox Stance**
   - **Description:** The orthodox stance is the most commonly used stance in boxing, primarily by right-handed fighters. In this stance, the boxer stands with their left foot forward and right foot back. The left hand is positioned as the lead hand, used primarily for jabs and quick punches, while the right hand is the power hand, utilized for stronger punches like crosses and hooks.

Tony Canzoneri standing in an orthodox stance

- **Advantages:**
  - **Straight Right Hand:** The right hand (power hand) is closer to the opponent, allowing for more forceful and precise right crosses and hooks. This positioning enhances the ability to land powerful punches and control the fight.
  - **Effective Jabbing:** The lead hand (left hand) is ideally positioned for jabs and quick, probing punches. This allows for effective range-finding and setting up combinations.
  - **Defensive Position:** The left foot is positioned closer to the opponent, facilitating quicker defensive movements and counter-attacks. This stance helps in managing distance and responding to the opponent's attacks.

2. **Southpaw Stance**
   - **Description:** The southpaw stance is used primarily by left-handed fighters. In this stance, the boxer stands with their right foot forward and left foot back. The right hand is the lead hand, used for jabs, while the left hand is the power hand, utilized for delivering powerful punches.
   - **Advantages:**
     - **Unorthodox Angles:** The southpaw stance provides a unique angle that can be challenging for opponents, particularly those accustomed to fighting orthodox boxers. This can create opportunities for landing punches that might otherwise be difficult to land.

BOXING STANCE AND FOOTWORK

Southpaw Stance

- **Powerful Left Hand:** The left hand (power hand) is positioned closer to the opponent, enhancing the ability to deliver powerful left crosses and hooks. This positioning can be advantageous for landing strong punches.
- **Defensive Advantages:** The right foot being closer to the opponent allows for better defensive positioning and counter-attacks. This stance can help in managing distance and creating openings.

Footwork Fundamentals: Moving In, Out, and Around the Ring

Footwork is a critical aspect of boxing, affecting how a boxer moves, positions themselves, and executes their strategy. Effective footwork enables a boxer to advance, retreat, and maneuver around the ring with precision. Here's a detailed look at the fundamental movements:

1. **Moving In (Advancing)**
    - **Purpose:** Advancing is essential for closing the distance between a boxer and their opponent. It allows a boxer to initiate attacks and capitalize on openings created by movement.

Advancing

- **Technique:**
    - **Step with the Lead Foot:** Begin by stepping forward with the lead foot (left foot for orthodox, right foot for southpaw). This movement

BOXING STANCE AND FOOTWORK

brings the boxer closer to the opponent while maintaining balance.

- o **Follow with the Rear Foot:** After moving the lead foot, bring the rear foot (right foot for orthodox, left foot for southpaw) up to maintain proper stance and balance. Ensure that both feet remain aligned and that weight is distributed evenly.
- o **Maintain Balance:** Keep your weight centered and avoid overcommitting. Proper balance is crucial to prevent being off-balance, which can leave you vulnerable to counter-attacks.

2. **Moving Out (Retreating)**

Back heel

- **Purpose:** Retreating is used to create distance and avoid incoming punches. It allows a boxer to regroup and reassess their strategy while staying out of range.
- **Technique:**
    - **Step Back with the Rear Foot:** Move the rear foot (right foot for orthodox, left foot for southpaw) backward first. This movement creates space and helps in evading punches.
    - **Follow with the Lead Foot:** Bring the lead foot (left foot for orthodox, right foot for southpaw) back to maintain balance and ensure proper alignment.
    - **Stay Low:** Maintain a low stance and keep your weight centered to remain balanced and agile while retreating. This helps in quickly transitioning back into an offensive stance if needed.

3. **Moving Around (Circling)**

Circling

- **Purpose:** Circling helps a boxer maneuver around their opponent, create angles, and avoid being cornered. It allows for strategic positioning and exploiting openings.
- **Technique:**
  - **Pivot on the Lead Foot:** To change direction, pivot on the lead foot (left foot for orthodox, right foot for southpaw). This movement facilitates turning and positioning without losing balance.
  - **Step with the Rear Foot:** Move the rear foot (right foot for orthodox, left foot for southpaw) to follow the pivot and maintain balance. Ensure that the movement is smooth and controlled.
  - **Use Small Steps:** Employ small, controlled steps to adjust positioning and create angles. This helps in maintaining control and staying within striking range while avoiding the opponent's punches.

Drills to Improve Stance and Footwork

Effective training drills can significantly enhance a boxer's stance and footwork. Here's a detailed guide to some valuable drills:

1. **Shadow Boxing**
   - **Purpose:** Shadow boxing allows boxers to practice their stance and footwork in a controlled environment. It helps in reinforcing muscle memory and improving technique.

Jack Dempsey shadow boxing in the ring

- **Drill:**
  - **Start in Your Stance:** Begin in your preferred stance and practice moving in, out, and around while maintaining proper balance. Focus on executing smooth and controlled movements.
  - **Incorporate Punches:** Add punches to your movements, practicing combinations while maintaining your stance and footwork. This integration helps in developing coordination between movement and striking.
  - **Visualize an Opponent:** Imagine an opponent's movements and practice adjusting your stance

BOXING STANCE AND FOOTWORK

and footwork accordingly. This visualization helps in preparing for real fight scenarios.

2. **Footwork Ladder Drills**
   - **Purpose:** Footwork ladder drills enhance speed, agility, and coordination. They are designed to improve quickness and precision in foot movements.
   - **Drill:**
     - **Set Up a Ladder:** Lay a ladder flat on the ground or use markers to create a ladder-like pattern. Ensure the ladder is placed in a clear space with enough room for movement.
     - **Perform Ladder Drills:** Practice various footwork patterns such as stepping in and out of each rung, moving laterally, and executing quick pivots. Focus on maintaining speed while executing precise movements.
     - **Focus on Technique:** Ensure that each step is deliberate and controlled. Proper form and technique are crucial for maximizing the benefits of the drill.

3. **Shadow Boxing with Movement**
   - **Purpose:** This drill combines shadow boxing with focused footwork practice, helping boxers integrate movement into their striking routines.
   - **Drill:**
     - **Move Around the Ring:** While shadow boxing, practice moving in, out, and around the imaginary ring. Focus on maintaining a solid stance and executing effective footwork.

Shadow boxing with movement

- ○ **Change Directions:** Incorporate quick changes in direction and angle to simulate real fight scenarios. Practice transitioning smoothly between offensive and defensive positions.
- ○ **Combine with Punches:** Add punches and defensive movements to your footwork practice. Focus on coordinating your strikes with your movement to improve overall performance.

4. **Partner Drills**
   - **Purpose:** Partner drills provide a more realistic practice environment, allowing boxers to test their stance and footwork against a moving opponent.

Partner Drills

- **Drill:**
  - **Controlled Sparring:** Engage in light sparring with a partner, focusing on maintaining your stance and using effective footwork. Practice advancing, retreating, and circling while responding to your partner's movements.
  - **Footwork Focus:** Have your partner move around and apply light pressure while you work on advancing, retreating, and circling. Emphasize maintaining proper balance and positioning.
  - **Feedback and Adjustment:** After the drill, discuss and analyze any issues with your stance and footwork with your partner. Use their feedback to make necessary adjustments and improve your technique.

5. **Cone Drills**
   - **Purpose:** Cone drills enhance agility, coordination, and the ability to change direction quickly. They are effective for improving overall footwork and movement.
   - **Drill:**
     - **Set Up Cones:** Place cones in various patterns on the floor, such as a zigzag or circular arrangement. Ensure the cones are spaced appropriately for the desired drill.

BOXING STANCE AND FOOTWORK

Cone Drills

- **Navigate the Course:** Practice moving through the cone course using different footwork patterns, such as shuffling, pivoting, and stepping. Focus on maintaining control and precision in your movements.

- **Increase Speed:** Gradually increase your speed while executing the drill. Ensure that you maintain proper form and technique as you progress.

Mastering boxing stance and footwork is essential for success in the ring. A solid stance provides the foundation for balance, power, and defense, while effective footwork enhances mobility and strategic positioning. By understanding the differences between orthodox and southpaw stances, practicing fundamental footwork techniques, and incorporating targeted drills into your training regimen, you can improve your overall performance. Consistent practice, attention to detail, and a focus on refining your stance and footwork will lead to greater success in both training and competition. With dedication and perseverance, you'll build a strong foundation for your boxing career and elevate your skills to new heights.

SECTION TWO

LEARNING THE BASICS

5

BASIC PUNCHES AND COMBINATIONS

IN BOXING, MASTERING THE FUNDAMENTAL PUNCHES and combinations is essential for developing a well-rounded skill set. This chapter covers the basic punches—jab, cross, hooks, and uppercuts—as well as their uses and how to combine them effectively. Understanding these elements will help you build a solid foundation for both offense and defense in the ring.

The Jab: The Most Important Punch

The jab is often referred to as the most important punch in boxing. It serves multiple purposes and is a critical component of a boxer's arsenal. Here's why the jab is so crucial:

- **Setting Up Combinations:** The jab is used to set up other punches and combinations. By landing a jab, you can disrupt your opponent's rhythm and create openings

for more powerful strikes.
- **Maintaining Distance:** The jab helps maintain distance between you and your opponent. It allows you to control the pace of the fight and keep your opponent at bay, preventing them from closing in or landing effective punches.

The Jab

- **Measuring Range:** The jab is an effective tool for measuring range. By consistently jabbing, you can gauge the distance between you and your opponent, ensuring that you stay within striking range for your

more powerful punches.
- **Defensive Tool:** The jab also serves as a defensive tool. A well-timed jab can disrupt your opponent's attacks and create opportunities for counter-punching. It can also be used to keep an opponent's head and body moving, making it harder for them to land clean shots.

Technique:

1. **Starting Position:** Begin in your stance with your hands up and your weight evenly distributed.
2. **Extension:** Extend your lead arm (left arm for orthodox, right arm for southpaw) straight out, rotating your fist so that the thumb is on top. Keep your elbow slightly bent to maintain control.
3. **Recoil:** Quickly retract your arm back to your guard position after the punch. This helps you stay protected and ready for the next move.
4. **Body Movement:** Use a slight pivot of the lead foot to generate power and maintain balance.

The Cross: Power and Precision

The cross is a powerful straight punch thrown with the rear hand. It's often used in combination with the jab to create effective attacks. Here's how to use the cross effectively:

- **Power Generation:** The cross is one of the most powerful punches in boxing due to the involvement of the rear hand and the rotation of the body. It can be used to deliver powerful, straight shots that can knock

down or disorient your opponent.
- **Precision:** A well-placed cross can target specific areas of your opponent's head or body, maximizing the impact of the punch. It's essential to aim accurately to ensure that the punch lands effectively.
- **Combination Punching:** The cross is often used in combination with other punches, such as the jab. This combination can break through an opponent's defense and create openings for follow-up punches.

The Cross Parry

Technique:

1. **Starting Position:** Begin in your stance with your hands up and your weight evenly distributed.

2. **Rotation:** Rotate your rear foot and hips to generate power as you extend your rear arm (right arm for orthodox, left arm for southpaw) straight toward your target.
3. **Extension:** Fully extend your rear arm while keeping your shoulder high to protect your chin. Aim to punch straight through your opponent's guard.
4. **Recoil:** Quickly retract your rear arm back to your guard position, ensuring that you maintain balance and readiness for the next move.

Hooks and Uppercuts: Adding Variety

Hooks and uppercuts add variety to your punching repertoire and are crucial for breaking through an opponent's guard. Here's a breakdown of each:

1. **Hooks:**

A Hook punch to the point of the jaw

- **Purpose:** Hooks are designed to target the side of your opponent's head or body. They can be devastating when delivered with proper technique and timing.
- **Technique:**
  1. **Starting Position:** Begin in your stance with your hands up and your weight evenly distributed.
  2. **Rotation:** Rotate your body and pivot on your lead foot (left foot for orthodox, right foot for southpaw) to generate power.
  3. **Extension:** Bend your arm at a 90-degree angle and swing it horizontally toward your target. Aim for the side of your opponent's head or body.
  4. **Recoil:** After landing the hook, quickly retract your arm and return to your guard position.

2. **Uppercuts:**

Uppercut

BASIC PUNCHES AND COMBINATIONS

- **Purpose:** Uppercuts are designed to target the chin or jaw of your opponent, often used to catch them off guard or to capitalize on openings created by other punches.
- **Technique:**
    5. **Starting Position:** Begin in your stance with your hands up and your weight evenly distributed.
    6. **Bend Your Knees:** Drop slightly by bending your knees to generate power from your legs.
    7. **Extension:** Punch upward with your lead or rear hand, aiming for your opponent's chin or jaw. Your elbow should remain close to your body.
    8. **Recoil:** Quickly retract your arm and return to your guard position, ready to defend or follow up with additional punches.

Basic Punch Combinations and Their Uses

Effective punch combinations are essential for breaking through an opponent's defense and creating openings for more powerful strikes. Here's a guide to some fundamental combinations and their uses:

1. **Jab-Cross (1-2)**
    - **Purpose:** This is one of the most basic and effective combinations. The jab (1) is used to disrupt your opponent's rhythm and create openings, while the cross (2) delivers a powerful follow-up punch.
    - **Application:** Use this combination to establish your jab and then capitalize on the opening created with the cross. It's effective for both initiating an attack and maintaining pressure on your opponent.

2. **Jab-Cross-Hook (1-2-3)**
   - **Purpose:** Adding a hook to the jab-cross combination introduces variety and can catch your opponent off guard.
   - **Application:** Start with the jab (1) and cross (2) to create an opening, then follow up with a hook (3) to target the side of your opponent's head or body. This combination is useful for breaking through defenses and setting up further attacks.
3. **Jab-Cross-Uppercut (1-2-5)**
   - **Purpose:** This combination uses the uppercut to exploit openings created by the jab and cross.
   - **Application:** Begin with the jab (1) and cross (2) to set up the uppercut (5). The uppercut is effective for targeting the chin or jaw, especially when your opponent's guard is lowered or compromised.
4. **Double Jab-Cross (1-1-2)**
   - **Purpose:** Throwing a double jab before the cross helps to close the distance and disrupt your opponent's defense.
   - **Application:** Use the double jab (1-1) to set up the cross (2). This combination is useful for breaking through a tight guard and landing a powerful punch.
5. **Hook-Cross-Hook (3-2-3)**
   - **Purpose:** This combination incorporates hooks to target the sides of your opponent's head or body, followed by a cross for added power.
   - **Application:** Start with a hook (3) to the head or body, follow with a cross (2) to exploit openings, and finish with another hook (3). This combination

BASIC PUNCHES AND COMBINATIONS

is effective for creating openings and maintaining offensive pressure.

6. **Uppercut-Hook-Cross (5-3-2)**

Uppercut-Hook-Cross

- **Purpose:** Combining an uppercut with hooks and a cross creates a dynamic and unpredictable attack.
- **Application:** Start with an uppercut (5) to target the chin, follow with a hook (3) to the side, and finish with a cross (2) for added power. This combination is useful for catching your opponent off guard and breaking through their defense.

Drills to Practice Punches and Combinations

1. **Shadow Boxing with Combinations**
   - **Purpose:** Shadow boxing allows you to practice punches and combinations in a controlled environment, focusing on technique and fluidity.
   - **Drill:**
     1. **Practice Combos:** Perform shadow boxing routines, incorporating various punches and combinations.
     2. **Focus on Form:** Pay attention to your stance, balance, and technique while executing the combinations.
     3. **Increase Speed:** Gradually increase your speed while maintaining proper technique and control.
2. **Heavy Bag Work**
   - **Purpose:** Using a heavy bag helps build power, endurance, and precision with punches and combinations.
   - **Drill:**
     4. **Perform Combinations:** Work on different combinations, focusing on power and accuracy.
     5. **Vary Intensity:** Alternate between high-intensity bursts and moderate-paced combinations to simulate different fight scenarios.
     6. **Maintain Form:** Ensure that you maintain proper technique and balance while working on the heavy bag.

BASIC PUNCHES AND COMBINATIONS

3. **Focus Mitt Drills**
   - **Purpose:** Focus mitts improve accuracy, timing, and coordination with a partner.
   - **Drill:**
     7. **Partner Practice:** Work with a partner who holds focus mitts while you execute various punches and combinations.
     8. **Adjust Speed:** Practice at different speeds, focusing on accuracy and reaction time.
     9. **Receive Feedback:** Use your partner's feedback to refine your technique and improve your combinations.
4. **Pad Work**
   - **Purpose:** Pad work with a coach or partner helps simulate real fight scenarios and improves combination execution.
   - **Drill:**
     10. **Execute Combinations:** Practice different combinations with pads, focusing on speed and precision.
     11. **Adjust Angles:** Work on executing combinations from various angles and distances.
     12. **Incorporate Movement:** Combine punches with footwork to enhance your ability to move in and out of range.

5. **Speed Bag Training**
   - **Purpose:** Speed bag training enhances hand-eye coordination and improves the speed of your punches.
   - **Drill:**
     13. **Practice Timing:** Work on hitting the speed bag with accurate timing and rhythm.
     14. **Incorporate Punches:** Combine speed bag training with punches and combinations to improve overall speed and coordination.
     15. **Increase Intensity:** Gradually increase the intensity and speed of your punches while maintaining proper technique.

Mastering the basic punches and combinations is crucial for any aspiring boxer. The jab, cross, hooks, and uppercuts form the core of your offensive arsenal, while effective combinations enable you to create openings and maintain pressure on your opponent. Through consistent practice and drills, you can enhance your technique, power, and precision, setting the stage for success in the ring. As you develop your skills, remember that perfecting these basics is the key to becoming a proficient and formidable boxer.

6

DEFENSIVE TECHNIQUES

IN BOXING, DEFENSE IS AS VITAL AS OFFENSE. THE ABILITY to effectively defend yourself against an opponent's attacks not only reduces the risk of getting hurt but also provides opportunities to launch counterattacks. This chapter delves deeply into key defensive techniques: blocking and parrying punches, slipping and ducking, rolling with punches, and counterpunching basics. Mastery of these techniques will enhance your defensive skills and overall boxing effectiveness.

Blocking and Parrying Punches

Blocking

Blocking Punches

Blocking is one of the most fundamental defensive techniques in boxing. It involves using your arms, gloves, and body to stop or deflect punches.

- **Purpose:** Blocking serves to absorb or deflect the force of an incoming punch, preventing it from landing cleanly. Effective blocking can neutralize your opponent's attacks and reduce the risk of injury.
- **Technique:**
  1. **Positioning:** Start in your boxing stance with your hands up and your elbows close to your body. Your gloves should be positioned near your face, with your elbows protecting your torso.

Blocking Stance

  2. **Forearm Blocks:** Use your forearms to block punches aimed at your head. For high punches,

raise your arms and use your forearms to deflect the punch. For body shots, lower your arms and use your elbows to shield your torso. Ensure that your arms are not rigid; a slight bend in the elbows helps absorb the impact.

Forearm Blocks

3. **Glove Blocks:** For punches targeting the head, use the palms of your gloves to absorb the impact. Keep your gloves close to your face, with your thumbs up and wrists straight. This position helps in absorbing the force and preventing it from landing on your chin or face.

Glove Blocks

4. **Body Blocks:** To block body shots, turn your torso slightly and use your gloves or forearms to absorb the impact. Ensure your elbows are close to your body to prevent punches from getting through.

- **Drills:**
  5. **Shadow Boxing with Blocks:** Practice shadow boxing while incorporating defensive blocks. Focus on maintaining proper form and transitioning smoothly between offense and defense. Visualize different types of punches and practice your blocking techniques accordingly.
  6. **Pad Work:** Work with a partner or coach who throws punches at you while you practice blocking. Emphasize timing and accuracy in your blocking technique. Ensure that you are not just reacting but also positioning yourself to follow up with counters.

Parrying Punches

Parrying Punches

Parrying involves redirecting an incoming punch away from its intended target. This technique is crucial for avoiding direct impact and creating opportunities for counterattacks.

- **Purpose:** Parrying allows you to deflect punches with minimal impact. By redirecting the punch, you can make

it miss or weaken its effect, making it easier to respond with counterattacks.
- **Technique:**
  1. **Light Touch:** Parrying requires a light touch with your glove or hand to redirect the punch. The goal is not to absorb the force but to guide it away from its target. Use a quick, flicking motion to achieve this.
  2. **Angle of Deflection:** Parry punches at an angle rather than directly. For example, if your opponent throws a jab, use a slight angle to redirect it to the side. This reduces the impact and makes it more challenging for your opponent to land a follow-up punch.
  3. **Follow Through:** After parrying, quickly return to your guard position. This ensures that you are ready to defend against further attacks and can immediately transition into offense if an opening is created.
- **Drills:**
  4. **Partner Parrying:** Practice with a partner who throws punches at you while you work on parrying. Focus on redirecting the punches and maintaining your defensive posture. Experiment with different angles and speeds to enhance your parrying skills.
  5. **Mirror Work:** Use a mirror to practice parrying techniques. Observe your movements and ensure that you are using proper form and angles. This helps in self-correction and improving accuracy.

Slipping and Ducking

Slipping and ducking are advanced defensive techniques that involve moving your head and body to avoid incoming punches.

Slipping

Slipping

Slipping involves moving your head and upper body to evade an incoming punch. It is particularly effective against punches aimed at the head.

- **Purpose:** Slipping helps you avoid getting hit by moving your head to one side or the other. This technique is useful for making punches miss and creating openings for counterattacks.
- **Technique:**
  1. **Head Movement:** Move your head to one side to avoid the punch. For a jab, slip to the outside of the punch, moving your head to the left if the jab is coming from your right. For a cross, slip to the inside or outside depending on the angle.
  2. **Body Rotation:** Rotate your torso slightly while slipping to enhance the evasion. This movement helps in maintaining balance and avoiding the full force of the punch.
  3. **Stay Low:** Maintain a slight bend in your knees to keep your center of gravity low. This helps in staying balanced and ready to counterattack if necessary.
- **Drills:**
  4. **Shadow Boxing with Slips:** Practice slipping punches while shadow boxing. Focus on maintaining proper head movement and body rotation. Visualize different types of punches and practice slipping them accordingly.
  5. **Slip Rope Drill:** Use a rope or string tied at head height to simulate incoming punches. Practice slipping under the rope to avoid the punch, ensuring you are moving your head and torso effectively.

Ducking

![Ducking]

Ducking

Ducking involves bending your knees and lowering your body to avoid punches aimed at your head. It is particularly effective against hooks and uppercuts.

- **Purpose:** Ducking allows you to evade punches by lowering your body. This technique is useful for avoiding hooks and uppercuts that target the head.
- **Technique:**
  1. **Bend Your Knees:** Lower your body by bending your knees, keeping your back straight. This movement helps in avoiding punches aimed at your head while maintaining balance.
  2. **Head Movement:** Keep your head down and to the side while ducking. This reduces the chances of getting hit by punches aimed at your head.
  3. **Maintain Balance:** Ensure that you stay balanced while ducking. Avoid leaning too far forward, which can make you vulnerable to counterattacks.
- **Drills:**
  4. **Duck and Counter:** Practice ducking under an imaginary punch and then quickly counterattacking. Focus on maintaining balance and transitioning smoothly between defense and offense.
  5. **Partner Ducking Drill:** Work with a partner who throws punches at you while you practice ducking. Emphasize timing, accuracy, and maintaining proper form.

DEFENSIVE TECHNIQUES

Rolling with Punches

![Rolling with Punches]

Rolling with Punches

Rolling with punches involves moving with the punch rather than resisting it directly. This technique helps in reducing the impact and maintaining balance.

- **Purpose:** Rolling with punches helps to absorb the force of the punch and reduces the risk of injury. It allows

you to stay balanced and ready for counterattacks.
- **Technique:**
  1. **Body Movement:** As a punch lands, roll your body in the direction of the punch. For example, if your opponent throws a right hook, roll your body to the right to dissipate the force.
  2. **Use of Shoulders:** Roll your shoulders to absorb and redirect the punch. This technique helps in maintaining balance and preparing for a counterattack.
  3. **Keep Your Guard Up:** Ensure that your hands and arms remain in a defensive position while rolling with punches. This helps in protecting yourself from follow-up punches and maintaining readiness for counterattacks.
- **Drills:**
  4. **Heavy Bag Work:** Practice rolling with punches while working on the heavy bag. Focus on minimizing the impact and maintaining proper form. Work on rolling with various types of punches, such as hooks and uppercuts.
  5. **Partner Drills:** Work with a partner who throws punches at you while you practice rolling with the punches. Emphasize timing, technique, and balance.

Counterpunching Basics

Counterpunching involves responding to your opponent's attack with a well-timed punch of your own. It is a crucial skill for turning defense into offense.

DEFENSIVE TECHNIQUES

Counterpunching

- **Purpose:** Counterpunching allows you to capitalize on openings created by your opponent's attacks. It helps in maintaining control of the fight and punishing your opponent for mistakes.
- **Technique:**
  1. **Timing:** Wait for your opponent to commit to a punch before countering. This ensures that you have a clear opening to land your counterpunch. Avoid countering too early or too late, as this can leave you vulnerable to further attacks.
  2. **Accuracy:** Aim for specific targets when counterpunching. Focus on hitting the openings created by your opponent's attack. Precision is crucial for effective counterpunching.
  3. **Combination:** Use counterpunches as part of

a combination. For example, you can counter a jab with a cross or a hook. Combining punches increases the effectiveness of your counterattacks and puts additional pressure on your opponent.
- **Drills:**
  4. **Counterpunch Practice:** Work with a partner who throws punches at you while you practice counterpunching. Focus on timing, accuracy, and execution. Experiment with different counterpunches and combinations to find what works best for you.
  5. **Shadow Boxing with Counters:** Incorporate counterpunches into your shadow boxing routine. Practice reacting to imaginary attacks and delivering effective counterpunches. Focus on maintaining proper technique and fluidity.

Defensive techniques are essential for any successful boxer. Mastering blocking, parrying, slipping, ducking, rolling with punches, and counterpunching will significantly enhance your defensive skills and overall boxing performance. Consistent practice and application of these techniques in training and sparring will help you stay protected, create openings, and effectively counter your opponent's attacks. As you develop your defensive skills, remember that a solid defense is the key to both surviving and thriving in the ring.

7

SPARRING AND DRILLS

SPARRING AND DRILLS ARE INTEGRAL ASPECTS OF boxing training, offering practical applications for techniques and essential improvements in skill and confidence. This chapter will thoroughly explore what to expect from sparring sessions, provide comprehensive drills to build technique and confidence, and explain the value of both shadow boxing and partner drills. By the end of this chapter, you will have a solid understanding of how to maximize your sparring and drill sessions to enhance your overall boxing abilities.

Introduction to Sparring: What to Expect

Sparring is a critical component of boxing training that simulates real fight conditions in a controlled environment. It is designed to help you apply techniques in real-time and assess your readiness for actual bouts. Understanding what to expect from sparring can help you approach it with the right mindset and make the most of these training sessions.

Purpose of Sparring

- **Real-Time Application:** Sparring provides an opportunity to practice techniques and strategies against a live opponent. It helps you understand how to apply skills learned in training and adjust them based on an opponent's reactions.
- **Ring Experience:** It allows you to experience the dynamics of a real fight, including managing distance, timing, and pressure. This experience is invaluable for developing ring awareness and adaptability.
- **Confidence Building:** Regular sparring helps build confidence in your abilities. By testing your skills against different opponents, you become more comfortable and self-assured in the ring.

What to Expect

- **Controlled Environment:** Sparring is usually conducted under the supervision of a coach or trainer who will set the parameters for the session. The intensity can vary, from light sparring focusing on technique to more intense sessions aimed at simulating fight conditions.
- **Communication with Your Partner:** Before sparring, discuss the goals and rules with your partner. Establish clear guidelines for the intensity of the session, such as focusing on technique, working on specific combinations, or testing endurance.
- **Focus on Technique:** During sparring, emphasize the application of techniques rather than trying to win. Use the session as a learning experience to refine your skills

and adapt to different styles and strategies.
- **Respect and Sportsmanship:** Approach sparring with respect for your partner. Understand that it is a mutual learning experience and avoid excessive aggression. Maintain good sportsmanship and use the opportunity to improve both your own skills and those of your partner.

Preparing for Sparring

- **Warm-Up:** A thorough warm-up is crucial before sparring to prepare your body for the physical demands of the session. This can include light jogging, dynamic stretching, and shadow boxing to increase your heart rate and loosen your muscles.
- **Gear Check:** Ensure that you have all the necessary protective gear, including headgear, gloves, mouthguard, and groin protector. Check that all equipment is in good condition and properly fitted to prevent injuries.

Drills to Build Technique and Confidence

Drills are essential for honing specific boxing skills and building confidence. They provide structured practice and allow you to focus on different aspects of your technique. Here, we will explore various drills designed to improve your boxing abilities and prepare you for sparring.

Shadow Boxing

- **Purpose:** Shadow boxing is a solo drill that helps you practice your techniques, footwork, and combinations

without a partner. It allows you to focus on form, fluidity, and visualization.
- **Technique:**
  - **Movement:** Practice moving around as if you are in a real fight. Incorporate different punches, combinations, and defensive maneuvers while maintaining balance and fluidity.
  - **Visualization:** Imagine an opponent in front of you and react to their movements. This mental exercise helps in developing your ability to respond to various scenarios and adapt your techniques accordingly.
  - **Mirror Work:** Use a mirror to observe your movements and technique. Ensure that your punches are executed with proper form and that your footwork is smooth and balanced.
- **Drills:**
  - **Combination Practice:** Focus on specific combinations of punches and practice them repeatedly. For example, work on jab-cross-hook or jab-uppercut combinations. This helps build muscle memory and confidence in executing these techniques.
  - **Footwork Integration:** Incorporate footwork into your shadow boxing routine. Practice moving in different directions, such as stepping forward, backward, and to the sides, while executing punches and defensive maneuvers. This helps in developing fluidity and coordination.

Heavy Bag Drills

Heavy bags

- **Purpose:** Heavy bag drills help in developing power, technique, and endurance. They provide a way to practice punching with resistance and simulate real fight conditions.
- **Technique:**
  - **Power Punching:** Focus on throwing powerful punches with proper technique. Utilize your whole body to generate force, and ensure that you are engaging your core and legs to maximize the impact of your punches.
  - **Movement:** Work on moving around the bag as you throw punches. Simulate different angles and

distances, and practice shifting your weight to enhance your attacking and defensive capabilities.
- **Drills:**
  - **Round-Based Workouts:** Perform heavy bag drills in rounds, similar to a fight. For example, do three-minute rounds with one-minute rest intervals. This helps build endurance and replicates the physical demands of a real fight.
  - **Technique-Focused Rounds:** Alternate between rounds focusing on specific techniques, such as power punching, precision, or combinations. For instance, spend one round working on powerful punches and another on improving accuracy and form.

Double-End Bag Drills

- **Purpose:** The double-end bag improves hand-eye coordination, timing, and reflexes. It provides a dynamic target that moves in response to your punches, enhancing your ability to hit moving targets.
- **Technique:**
  - **Timing and Accuracy:** Work on hitting the bag with precise timing. The bag's movement will challenge your accuracy and reaction speed. Focus on landing clean, effective punches while maintaining balance.
  - **Combination Practice:** Practice different punch combinations while the bag is in motion. This helps in developing the ability to land punches effectively while dealing with a moving target.

- **Drills:**
  - **Speed and Rhythm:** Focus on hitting the bag quickly and with rhythm. Develop a consistent pace and timing to improve your speed and accuracy.
  - **Defensive Integration:** Incorporate defensive techniques, such as slipping and rolling, into your double-end bag drills. Practice avoiding punches while maintaining offensive pressure.

Partner Drills for Timing and Reaction

Partner drills are essential for developing timing, reaction, and the ability to respond to an opponent's movements. These drills help you practice techniques in a dynamic environment and improve your sparring performance.

Mitt drills

Mitt Work

- **Purpose:** Mitt work involves practicing punches and combinations with a coach or partner holding pads. It helps in improving accuracy, timing, and technique.
- **Technique:**
  - **Focus on Precision:** Aim for specific targets on the pads held by your coach or partner. Ensure that your punches are accurate and well-timed.
  - **Combination Practice:** Work on different combinations of punches, such as jab-cross-hook or uppercut-cross-hook. Your partner will call out combinations or move the pads to simulate various scenarios.
- **Drills:**
  - **Speed and Power:** Alternate between fast, explosive punches and powerful, deliberate punches. This helps in developing both speed and power in your attacks.
  - **Defensive Integration:** Incorporate defensive techniques, such as slipping and rolling, into your mitt work. Practice moving between offense and defense smoothly to enhance your overall boxing skills.

Reaction Drills

- **Purpose:** Reaction drills help improve your ability to respond quickly to an opponent's movements. These drills enhance your defensive and counterpunching skills.

Reaction Drills

- **Technique:**
  - **Randomized Attacks:** Have a partner throw punches at you unpredictably while you practice defending and counterattacking. This helps in developing quick reactions and adaptability.
  - **Response Time:** Focus on improving your response time to various attacks. Practice reacting quickly to different types of punches and movements, ensuring that you can adjust your defense and counter effectively.
- **Drills:**
  - **Focus Mitt Drills:** Practice reacting to different types of punches while your partner or coach holds focus mitts. The unpredictability of the mitts helps simulate real fight conditions and improves your reaction time.

- **Slip and Counter:** Work on slipping punches and immediately countering with your own attacks. This drill helps in developing the ability to capitalize on openings created by defensive movements.

Sparring and drills are crucial for developing and refining your boxing skills. Understanding what to expect from sparring sessions and incorporating a variety of drills into your training routine will significantly enhance your technique, confidence, and overall boxing performance. By regularly practicing shadow boxing, heavy bag work, double-end bag drills, and partner drills, you will build the skills needed for effective sparring and real fight conditions. Consistent practice and application of these techniques will lead to a more well-rounded and proficient boxer, ready to face the challenges of the ring.

SECTION THREE

CONDITIONING AND TRAINING

8

PHYSICAL CONDITIONING FOR BOXERS

PHYSICAL CONDITIONING FORMS THE BACKBONE OF effective boxing training. It is not just about building strength and endurance but also about ensuring that every part of your body works optimally to support your boxing skills. This chapter delves into the various facets of physical conditioning that are crucial for boxers, including cardiovascular fitness, strength training, flexibility, mobility, and recovery. Each of these components plays a pivotal role in enhancing your performance and ensuring long-term success in the sport.

The Importance of Cardiovascular Fitness

Cardiovascular fitness is crucial for boxers as it impacts your stamina, recovery, and overall in-ring performance. An effective cardiovascular system ensures that you can sustain high levels of activity throughout a match and recover efficiently between rounds.

1. Benefits of Cardiovascular Fitness

- **Endurance:** Cardiovascular fitness is integral to maintaining energy levels throughout extended periods of physical exertion. For a boxer, this means being able to keep up the pace, throw punches effectively, and maintain defensive strategies for the full duration of a fight.
- **Recovery:** A well-developed cardiovascular system allows your body to recover more quickly from high-intensity activities. Improved recovery means you can perform better in subsequent rounds and minimize fatigue.
- **Efficiency:** A strong cardiovascular system enhances the efficiency of oxygen delivery to your muscles. This is critical for sustaining high-intensity efforts and ensuring that you can recover and continue performing at your best.

2. Cardiovascular Training Methods

- **Steady-State Cardio:** Engaging in steady-state cardio activities such as jogging, cycling, or swimming at a moderate intensity helps build endurance. Aim for 30 to 45 minutes of steady-state cardio sessions, 3 to 4 times per week. This type of training improves overall cardiovascular health and supports your base level of fitness.
- **Interval Training:** High-Intensity Interval Training (HIIT) alternates between periods of intense exercise and lower-intensity recovery. This method enhances cardiovascular capacity and simulates the bursts of

activity and recovery seen in boxing. For example, perform sprints for 30 seconds followed by a 1-minute jog or walk, and repeat for 20 to 30 minutes.
- **Jump Rope:** Skipping rope is a highly effective cardiovascular exercise that also improves coordination, agility, and footwork. Include various jump rope techniques such as single-leg jumps, double-unders, and high knees to enhance your cardiovascular conditioning and mimic the footwork required in boxing.

3. Incorporating Cardio into Your Training

- **Warm-Up:** Use cardiovascular exercises as part of your warm-up routine to prepare your body for more intense training. This helps increase your heart rate, warm up your muscles, and improve your overall performance.
- **Variety:** Include a mix of steady-state cardio, interval training, and sport-specific exercises to keep your workouts engaging and effective. This variety ensures a comprehensive approach to cardiovascular fitness.
- **Consistency:** Adhere to a consistent cardio regimen to build and maintain endurance. Regularly evaluate and adjust the intensity and duration of your cardio workouts based on your fitness goals and progress.

Strength Training for Boxers

Strength training is vital for enhancing a boxer's power, speed, and resilience. It improves the force of your punches, supports faster and more efficient movement, and reduces the risk of injuries.

1. Benefits of Strength Training

- **Power and Explosiveness:** Strength training develops the power behind your punches and overall athletic performance. Stronger muscles contribute to generating more force and explosive movements, which are essential for effective striking and rapid footwork.
- **Injury Prevention:** A well-structured strength training program enhances muscle and joint stability, which reduces the risk of injuries. Strength training also helps correct muscle imbalances, improving overall body mechanics and reducing the likelihood of strains and sprains.
- **Enhanced Performance:** Increased muscle strength contributes to better control and stability during punches and defensive maneuvers. Stronger muscles also improve your overall agility and ability to handle physical stress during a fight.

2. Key Strength Training Exercises

- **Upper Body:**
    - **Push-Ups:** Push-ups are an excellent exercise for building strength in the chest, shoulders, and triceps. Variations such as standard push-ups, diamond push-ups, and decline push-ups target different muscle groups and enhance overall upper body strength.
    - **Pull-Ups/Chin-Ups:** These exercises strengthen the back, shoulders, and arms. Different grips (overhand, underhand) emphasize various muscles and improve upper body pulling strength.

- **Dumbbell/Barbell Presses:** These exercises, including bench presses and overhead presses, develop strength in the chest, shoulders, and triceps. They are crucial for increasing punching power and upper body strength.
- **Punching Drills with Resistance:** Incorporate resistance bands or weights into punching drills to enhance the power and endurance of your punches. This exercise simulates the force required during actual punches and improves muscle conditioning.

• **Lower Body:**
- **Squats:** Squats are fundamental for strengthening the quadriceps, hamstrings, and glutes. Variations include bodyweight squats, goblet squats, and barbell squats, each contributing to lower body strength and power.
- **Lunges:** Lunges improve leg strength, balance, and coordination. Perform forward, reverse, and lateral lunges to target different muscle groups and enhance lower body stability.
- **Deadlifts:** Deadlifts build overall lower body and core strength. Focus on proper form to prevent injuries and maximize the benefits of this compound exercise.

• **Core:**
- **Planks:** Planks are essential for core stability and endurance. Perform front planks and side planks to strengthen the core muscles, which support overall body strength and stability.
- **Russian Twists:** This exercise targets the oblique muscles and improves rotational power. Use a

weight or medicine ball to add resistance and enhance core strength.

- **Leg Raises:** Leg raises build lower abdominal strength and improve core stability. Perform this exercise with controlled movements to maximize effectiveness.

Flexibility and Mobility Workouts

Flexibility and mobility are critical for maintaining an optimal range of motion, preventing injuries, and enhancing overall performance. Boxers need to be agile and mobile to execute techniques effectively and adapt to dynamic fight conditions.

Flexibility Exercises

2. Flexibility Exercises

- **Static Stretching:** Static stretching involves holding stretches for 20 to 30 seconds to improve muscle flexibility. Focus on major muscle groups such as the hamstrings, quadriceps, calves, and shoulders.
  - **Hamstring Stretch:** Sit on the floor with one leg extended and reach for your toes. Switch legs after 20 to 30 seconds to enhance flexibility in the hamstrings.
  - **Quadriceps Stretch:** Stand on one leg, grab your ankle, and pull it towards your glutes. Switch legs after 20 to 30 seconds to stretch the quadriceps effectively.
  - **Shoulder Stretch:** Cross one arm over your chest and use the opposite arm to gently pull it closer. Switch arms after 20 to 30 seconds to stretch the shoulder muscles.
- **Dynamic Stretching:** Dynamic stretching involves performing movements that mimic your boxing techniques to prepare your body for activity. This type of stretching increases blood flow and warms up your muscles.
  - **Leg Swings:** Swing one leg forward and backward, then side to side. Repeat with the other leg to enhance hip flexibility and range of motion.
  - **Arm Circles:** Perform circular motions with your arms to warm up your shoulder joints and muscles. This exercise helps improve shoulder flexibility and mobility.

Mobility Exercises

3. Mobility Workouts

- **Foam Rolling:** Foam rolling, or self-myofascial release, reduces muscle tightness and improves mobility. Use a foam roller to target areas such as the back, legs, and arms, applying gentle pressure to release muscle knots and enhance flexibility.
- **Joint Mobility Exercises:** Perform exercises that focus on joint movement and flexibility, such as hip circles,

shoulder rolls, and ankle rotations. These exercises improve the mobility of specific joints and support overall movement quality.

- **Yoga:** Incorporating yoga into your routine enhances flexibility, balance, and relaxation. Focus on poses that stretch and strengthen key muscle groups used in boxing, such as downward dog, warrior poses, and pigeon pose.

Rest and Recovery: Avoiding Overtraining

Rest and recovery are essential components of any training program. Proper recovery allows your body to repair and strengthen, reducing the risk of overtraining and injury.

1. Importance of Rest and Recovery

- **Muscle Repair:** During rest, muscles repair and grow stronger. Adequate rest allows your body to recover from intense workouts, rebuild muscle tissue, and improve overall strength.
- **Injury Prevention:** Proper recovery reduces the risk of overuse injuries and burnout. It helps maintain overall physical health and prevents training-related injuries.
- **Performance Enhancement:** Adequate rest improves overall performance by ensuring that you are well-rested and prepared for subsequent training sessions and fights. Rest supports better focus, energy levels, and physical readiness.

2. Strategies for Effective Recovery

- **Rest Days:** Incorporate rest days into your training schedule to allow your body to recover. Aim for at least

one full rest day per week, and consider active recovery activities such as light stretching or walking on other rest days to maintain mobility.
- **Sleep:** Prioritize quality sleep to support muscle recovery and overall well-being. Aim for 7 to 9 hours of sleep per night and establish a regular sleep routine to promote better rest and recovery.
- **Nutrition:** Support recovery with a balanced diet rich in protein, carbohydrates, and healthy fats. Proper nutrition aids muscle repair, replenishes energy stores, and supports overall recovery. Consider post-workout meals and snacks that include protein and carbohydrates to enhance recovery.
- **Hydration:** Stay well-hydrated to support muscle function and recovery. Drink plenty of water before, during, and after workouts to prevent dehydration and maintain optimal performance.

Consistent effort and attention to each of these areas will lead to significant improvements in your boxing capabilities and long-term success in the sport.

9

NUTRITION AND DIET

NUTRITION IS NOT JUST ABOUT EATING THE RIGHT foods; it's a science and an art that fuels a boxer's performance, aids in recovery, and maintains overall health. For boxers, every meal is an opportunity to enhance training outcomes, optimize fight performance, and ensure swift recovery.

The Role of Nutrition in Boxing Performance

Nutrition serves as the foundation for athletic performance, influencing how well a boxer performs in training and competition. Proper dietary practices ensure that the body has sufficient energy, recovers efficiently, and remains in peak physical condition.

1. Energy Supply

- **Carbohydrates:** Carbohydrates are the primary source of energy for high-intensity exercise. They are broken down into glucose, which is stored as glycogen in muscles and the liver. This glycogen is utilized during strenuous workouts and fights. Complex carbohydrates, which include foods like whole grains, vegetables, and legumes, provide a steady release of energy and are crucial for maintaining stamina.

- **Complex Carbohydrates:** Opt for foods such as brown rice, quinoa, whole-wheat pasta, and oats. These carbohydrates are digested slowly, providing sustained energy over long periods.
- **Simple Carbohydrates:** Foods like fruits, honey, and sports drinks offer quick energy boosts and can be particularly useful during or after intense training sessions for rapid glycogen replenishment.

- **Proteins:** Proteins play a critical role in muscle repair and growth. After rigorous training, muscle fibers undergo stress and need proteins to repair and build new muscle tissue. Essential amino acids, which are the building blocks of protein, must be supplied through diet.
    - **High-Quality Proteins:** Include sources such as lean meats (chicken, turkey), fish, eggs, dairy products, and plant-based proteins (tofu, legumes). Protein should constitute 10-35% of your daily caloric intake to support muscle recovery and growth.
    - **Protein Timing:** Consume protein-rich foods or supplements within 30 minutes to an hour after training to optimize muscle repair and recovery. Examples include a protein shake with a banana or grilled chicken with a side of vegetables.
- **Fats:** Fats are essential for energy, especially during prolonged exercise. They also support cell function, hormone production, and the absorption of fat-soluble

vitamins. Healthy fats should be included in the diet but in moderation.

- **Types of Fats:** Focus on unsaturated fats found in foods such as avocados, nuts, seeds, and olive oil. Limit saturated fats from sources like red meats and processed foods to prevent adverse health effects.
- **Inclusion:** Incorporate sources of healthy fats into your meals, such as adding nuts to yogurt or using olive oil for cooking.

2. Nutrient Timing

- **Pre-Training:** A balanced pre-training meal helps fuel your workout. Aim for a meal that is rich in carbohydrates and moderate in protein, consumed about 1-2 hours before exercise. Avoid high-fat or high-fiber foods that might cause digestive discomfort.
    - **Examples:** A bowl of oatmeal with berries, a whole-grain sandwich with turkey and vegetables, or a smoothie made with yogurt and fruit.
- **Post-Training:** After training, your body needs to replenish glycogen stores and repair muscle tissue. A meal or snack that includes both carbohydrates and protein is ideal for recovery.
    - **Examples:** A protein shake with a banana, a serving of Greek yogurt with honey and fruit, or a meal of grilled chicken with quinoa and steamed vegetables.
- **Throughout the Day:** Eating balanced meals and snacks throughout the day helps maintain energy levels and supports continuous recovery. Aim for a diet that includes a mix of carbohydrates, proteins, and fats.

- **Examples:** Regular meals could include a breakfast of eggs and avocado toast, a lunch of fish tacos with a side of black beans, and a snack of apple slices with almond butter.

3. Hydration

- **Importance of Hydration:** Proper hydration is critical for maintaining performance and overall health. Dehydration can lead to decreased endurance, reduced strength, and impaired recovery.
    - **Daily Intake:** Aim to drink at least 8-10 glasses (2-2.5 liters) of water each day. Adjust intake based on individual needs, training intensity, and climate conditions.
    - **Electrolytes:** During intense exercise, electrolyte levels can drop. Consuming beverages that contain electrolytes, such as sports drinks or coconut water, can help maintain fluid balance and prevent dehydration.
- **Hydration Strategies:**
    - **Before Exercise:** Drink plenty of water in the hours leading up to a workout. Aim to hydrate well before starting any intense physical activity.
    - **During Exercise:** For prolonged or high-intensity workouts, sip on water or an electrolyte-rich drink to stay hydrated.
    - **After Exercise:** Rehydrate with water and consider an electrolyte drink if your training was particularly intense or lengthy.

Pre-Fight Nutrition and Hydration

Effective nutrition and hydration strategies before a fight are critical for peak performance. Your choices leading up to the fight can impact your energy levels, strength, and overall readiness.

1. Carbohydrate Loading

- **Purpose:** Carbohydrate loading increases glycogen stores in muscles, providing extra energy for the fight. Begin this process 2-3 days before the fight.
- **Implementation:** Increase carbohydrate intake to 70% of your daily calories in the days leading up to the fight. Opt for high-carb, low-fiber foods to minimize digestive discomfort. Examples include white rice, pasta, and bread.

2. Timing

- **Pre-Fight Meal:** Eat a balanced meal about 3-4 hours before the fight. This meal should be rich in carbohydrates, moderate in protein, and low in fats and fiber to ensure optimal digestion and energy. Examples include a whole-grain sandwich with lean meat or a bowl of pasta with chicken.
- **Pre-Fight Snack:** If needed, consume a light snack 30-60 minutes before the fight to maintain energy levels. Options like a banana, a small energy bar, or a sports drink can provide a quick boost without causing discomfort.

3. Hydration

- **Pre-Fight Hydration:** Maintain proper hydration in the days before the fight. Drink water regularly and consider electrolyte-rich beverages to keep fluid levels balanced.
- **During the Fight:** Ensure access to water during breaks if the fight is long or involves multiple rounds. Follow any specific hydration strategies recommended by your coach or nutritionist.

Adopting these nutritional principles helps you stay at the top of your game and achieve your boxing goals.

SECTION FOUR

ADVANCED TECHNIQUES AND STRATEGY

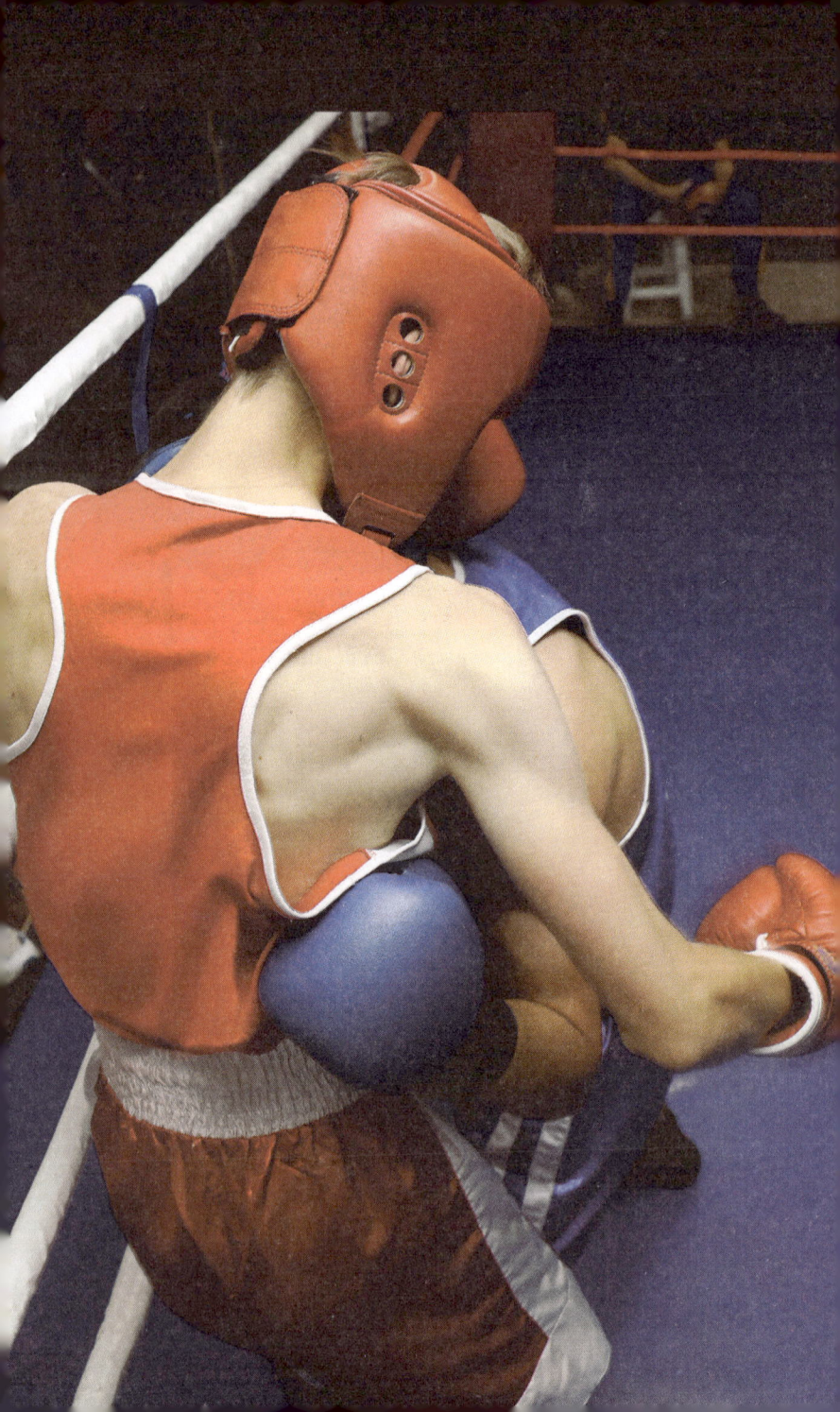

10

ADVANCED PUNCHING TECHNIQUES

ADVANCED PUNCHING TECHNIQUES ARE ESSENTIAL for developing a sophisticated and effective boxing style. As you advance from fundamental punches to more complex techniques, you'll enhance your ability to control the pace of the fight, exploit your opponent's weaknesses, and deliver powerful, strategic strikes. This chapter provides an in-depth exploration of advanced punching techniques, including the overhand right and left hook, body shots, setting up punches with fakes and feints, and effective punching combinations.

The Overhand Right and Left Hook

Advanced punches like the overhand right and left hook are crucial for breaking through defenses and delivering significant damage. These punches are powerful tools that require both technical precision and strategic application.

1. The Overhand Right

- **Technique and Execution**
    - **Positioning:** Begin in your orthodox stance with your feet shoulder-width apart. The overhand right is thrown with the dominant hand and is designed to come over and around your opponent's guard.
    - **Movement:** Initiate the punch by slightly shifting your weight to your back foot and rotating your torso. Your arm should execute a looping motion, coming over the opponent's guard. Aim for the target area, typically the head or upper body. Your punch should be delivered with force while maintaining balance and stability.
    - **Follow-Through:** After executing the punch, your body should rotate fully to maximize power. Be prepared to quickly return to your defensive stance or move to evade any potential counters from your opponent.
- **Tips for Mastery**
    - **Power Generation:** Utilize your entire body to generate power, not just your arm. Engage your core and legs to add force to the punch. The effectiveness of the overhand right relies on the synergy of your body's movement.
    - **Defense:** Keep your non-punching hand up to protect your face and avoid leaving yourself exposed. A well-timed overhand right can break through high guards and exploit forward movements.
- **Usage and Strategy**
    - **Countering:** The overhand right is particularly

ADVANCED PUNCHING TECHNIQUES

effective against opponents with high guards or those advancing toward you. It can also be used to counter a jab or an opponent's forward momentum.
- **Surprise Factor:** The overhand right's looping trajectory can catch opponents off-guard, especially if they anticipate a straight punch or are focused on defending against other strikes.

2. The Left Hook

- **Technique and Execution**
    - **Positioning:** In an orthodox stance, the left hook is delivered with your lead hand. This punch targets the side of your opponent's head or body.
    - **Movement:** Rotate your body and pivot your left foot as you throw the hook. Your elbow should be bent at approximately 90 degrees, and your fist should travel horizontally. Aim for the side of the opponent's head or ribs, depending on the angle and positioning.
    - **Follow-Through:** Ensure that your punch is executed with fluid motion and that you return quickly to your stance. A well-placed hook can cause significant damage and create openings for further attacks.
- **Tips for Mastery**
    - **Accuracy:** Focus on targeting vulnerable areas like the side of the head or ribs. Precision in landing the hook is crucial for maximizing impact and effectiveness.
    - **Defense:** Maintain a balanced stance and keep your right hand up to protect against counterattacks.

Proper technique will help prevent leaving yourself open to retaliation.
- **Usage and Strategy**
  - **Breaking Defense:** The left hook is effective for exploiting openings on the side or disrupting an opponent's defensive posture. It's particularly useful when the opponent is trying to evade a straight punch or when they are preparing to counter.
  - **Combination Punching:** Integrate the left hook with other punches, such as jabs or crosses, to create openings and overwhelm your opponent's defense.

Body Shots: Targeting the Midsection

Body shots are critical for weakening your opponent, reducing their stamina, and setting up opportunities for head shots. Effective body punching can disrupt your opponent's rhythm and force them to lower their guard.

1. Types of Body Shots

- **Straight Body Shot**
  - **Technique:** The straight body shot is delivered directly to the midsection, targeting areas such as the solar plexus or stomach. Initiate the punch by stepping forward and throwing a direct strike with your dominant hand.
  - **Execution:** Engage your core and use your body weight to drive power into the punch. Maintain a short, controlled motion to ensure precision and avoid overextending.

- **Hooks to the Body**
  - **Technique:** Body hooks target the ribs or liver. To execute a body hook, rotate your torso and pivot your feet while throwing the punch with a bent elbow.
  - **Execution:** Aim for the side of your opponent's ribcage or liver. A well-placed hook can cause significant pain and disrupt their ability to breathe effectively.
- **Uppercuts to the Body**
  - **Technique:** The uppercut to the body is an upward punch aimed at the midsection, often targeting the opponent's solar plexus or chin.
  - **Execution:** Start with a slight bend in your knees and throw the punch upward. Engage your legs to generate power and aim for the opponent's midsection or chin.

2. Effectiveness of Body Shots

- **Stamina Reduction:** Body shots can significantly sap your opponent's energy and reduce their overall stamina. Consistent body punching can weaken their ability to move and respond effectively.
- **Defense Disruption:** Targeting the body forces your opponent to lower their guard or adjust their stance, creating openings for head shots or further attacks. Body shots can break down their defensive posture and make them more vulnerable to additional strikes.

Setting Up Punches: Fakes and Feints

Fakes and feints are strategic tools used to mislead your

opponent and create openings for effective punches. Mastering these techniques can enhance your ability to land clean, powerful strikes and maintain control over the fight.

1. Understanding Fakes and Feints

- **Fake:** A fake involves simulating a punch or movement to provoke a defensive reaction from your opponent. The goal is to make them commit to a defense that you can then exploit with a real punch.
- **Feint:** A feint is a subtle movement or gesture that misleads your opponent about your intended punch or direction. It creates openings by causing your opponent to react prematurely, allowing you to capitalize on their response.

2. Techniques for Effective Fakes and Feints

- **Jab Feint**
  - **Execution:** Use a quick jab motion to create the illusion of an incoming punch. This can disrupt your opponent's guard and create an opportunity for a more powerful attack.
  - **Tips:** Make the jab feint realistic and convincing. Observe your opponent's reaction and follow up with a real punch or combination based on their response.
- **Shoulder Feint**
  - **Execution:** Move your shoulder or upper body as if preparing to throw a punch. This creates the appearance of an imminent attack, leading your opponent to react defensively.

ADVANCED PUNCHING TECHNIQUES

  - **Tips:** Combine the shoulder feint with actual punches to maintain unpredictability. The feint should be subtle yet effective to deceive your opponent.
- **Head Feint**
  - **Execution:** Use head movement to simulate an attack and create openings. Move your head slightly in one direction to make your opponent anticipate a punch from that angle.
  - **Tips:** Practice head feints to integrate them smoothly into your boxing style. Use them to disrupt your opponent's timing and create opportunities for real punches.

3. Applying Fakes and Feints

- **Creating Openings:** Utilize fakes and feints to provoke defensive reactions and create openings for effective strikes. By misleading your opponent, you can exploit their vulnerabilities and land powerful punches.
- **Combining Techniques:** Integrate fakes and feints with actual punches to enhance your overall strategy. Combining these techniques with real attacks keeps your opponent off-balance and uncertain about your next move.

Punching in Combinations: Creating Openings

Punching combinations are crucial for overwhelming your opponent and creating openings. Effective combinations require fluid execution, strategic variation, and the ability to adapt to your opponent's reactions.

1. Basic Combination Principles

- **Flow and Rhythm:** Develop a smooth flow between punches to maintain pressure and create openings. A well-timed combination can disrupt your opponent's defensive rhythm and increase the likelihood of landing effective strikes.
- **Variation:** Mix different types of punches, such as jabs, hooks, and uppercuts, to keep your opponent guessing and prevent them from predicting your next move.
- **Power and Precision:** Balance power and precision in your combinations. Accurate punches targeting specific areas can deliver effective damage while maintaining proper technique.

2. Common Punching Combinations

- **Jab-Cross-Hook**
  - **Execution:** Start with a jab to gauge distance and disrupt your opponent's guard. Follow with a cross to deliver power, and finish with a hook to capitalize on openings created by the previous punches.
  - **Application:** This combination is effective for breaking through defenses and creating openings. Use it to set up additional punches or follow-up attacks, and adjust based on your opponent's response.
- **Double Jab-Cross**
  - **Execution:** Throw two quick jabs in succession to create a defensive opening. Follow with a powerful cross to capitalize on the disruption caused by the jabs.

- **Application:** The double jab helps close the distance and set up the cross. This combination is useful for overwhelming your opponent and creating openings for further strikes.
- **Hook-Uppercut-Hook**
  - **Execution:** Begin with a hook to target the opponent's head or body. Follow with an uppercut to catch them off-guard, and finish with another hook to exploit the opening created by the previous punches.
  - **Application:** This combination is effective for breaking through defenses and targeting different angles. Use it to create opportunities for finishing punches or to disrupt your opponent's rhythm.

By focusing on techniques such as the overhand right, left hook, body shots, and the strategic use of fakes and feints, you can develop a powerful and versatile punching arsenal.

11

ADVANCED DEFENSIVE TACTICS

ADVANCED DEFENSIVE TACTICS ARE CRUCIAL FOR a boxer seeking to elevate their skills and outmaneuver opponents. A well-rounded defensive strategy not only prevents you from taking damage but also positions you to counterattack effectively. This chapter delves into advanced defensive techniques, including mastering the shoulder roll, advanced slipping and countering, using angles to avoid punches, and clinching and fighting inside. Developing these skills will enhance your defensive capabilities and enable you to control the flow of the fight.

Mastering the Shoulder Roll

The shoulder roll is a sophisticated defensive maneuver that helps you deflect punches and create openings for counterattacks. It involves precise timing and a solid understanding of your opponent's offensive patterns.

ADVANCED DEFENSIVE TACTICS

1. Technique and Execution

- **Positioning:** Begin in your orthodox stance with your feet shoulder-width apart and your hands up. The shoulder roll involves rolling your dominant shoulder forward and inward to absorb and deflect punches. Your chin should be tucked behind your shoulder to protect against head strikes.
- **Movement:** As your opponent throws a punch, pivot slightly on your back foot and rotate your shoulder to deflect the incoming strike. This motion creates a shield that redirects the punch away from your head or body. Maintain your balance and be ready to transition into an offensive position.
- **Follow-Through:** After deflecting the punch, use the momentary gap to deliver a counterpunch. The shoulder roll not only deflects punches but also sets you up for quick, effective counters. Utilize the brief period when your opponent is off-balance to land a decisive strike.

2. Tips for Mastery

- **Timing and Anticipation:** Perfecting the shoulder roll requires impeccable timing. Anticipate your opponent's punches by observing their body language and movement. Practice rolling your shoulder in response to various types of attacks to improve your reaction time.
- **Head and Body Movement:** Combine the shoulder roll with head and body movement to further enhance your defensive capabilities. Moving your head away from the punch's trajectory and adjusting your body position can make you more elusive and harder to hit.

- **Stance and Balance:** Ensure that your stance remains stable while performing the shoulder roll. A balanced stance allows you to maintain control and quickly switch between defense and offense. Work on your footwork to complement the shoulder roll and enhance overall effectiveness.

3. Usage and Strategy

- **Deflecting Straight Punches:** The shoulder roll is particularly effective against straight punches, such as jabs and crosses. By redirecting these punches off your shoulder, you can minimize their impact and create openings for counters.
- **Breaking Through Guards:** Use the shoulder roll to break through high guards or defensive stances. By deflecting punches and moving your opponent's guard, you can create opportunities to land effective strikes.

Advanced Slipping and Countering

Slipping is a defensive technique that involves moving your head and upper body to evade punches while setting up counterattacks. Advanced slipping requires precise movements and an understanding of your opponent's attack patterns.

1. Technique and Execution

- **Slipping:** To slip a punch, move your head and torso to the side or backward. This motion causes the punch to miss your target. Ensure that you remain in a position to deliver a counterpunch immediately after slipping.

- **Advanced Slipping:** Practice advanced slipping by incorporating multiple slips and head movements. Train to evade a series of punches by moving in different directions and angles. This technique helps you avoid getting caught in predictable patterns.
- **Counterattacking:** After slipping a punch, quickly follow up with a counterpunch. Utilize the opening created by the slip to deliver a decisive strike. The goal is to capitalize on your opponent's momentary vulnerability and score effective punches.

2. Tips for Mastery

- **Head Movement Coordination:** Combine slipping with head movement to enhance your defensive skills. Practice moving your head off the centerline and away from the punch's trajectory. This coordination reduces the chances of being hit and improves your overall defense.
- **Footwork Integration:** Integrate slipping with footwork to maintain balance and positioning. Effective footwork allows you to move and create angles while avoiding punches. Practice slipping while moving in different directions to develop a well-rounded defensive strategy.
- **Drills and Sparring:** Work with a partner to practice slipping and countering drills. Focus on timing, accuracy, and fluidity in your movements. Sparring sessions provide valuable experience in applying these techniques against live opponents.

3. Usage and Strategy

- **Avoiding Various Punches:** Advanced slipping techniques are effective for avoiding straight punches, hooks, and uppercuts. Use slipping to evade different types of attacks and disrupt your opponent's offensive strategy.
- **Creating Openings:** Utilize the openings created by slipping to deliver counterpunches. Advanced slipping can break your opponent's rhythm and create opportunities for effective strikes.

Using Angles to Avoid Punches

Creating and exploiting angles is a key defensive strategy that involves positioning yourself to avoid punches while setting up opportunities for counterattacks. By moving at different angles, you can make it challenging for your opponent to land effective strikes.

1. Technique and Execution

- **Creating Angles:** Move laterally or pivot your body to create angles that make it difficult for your opponent to hit you. For instance, pivoting to the left can help you avoid a right-hand punch while positioning yourself to counter from a more advantageous angle.
- **Footwork:** Use lateral movement and pivoting to create and exploit angles. Effective footwork enables you to shift your position while maintaining balance and control. Practice moving in different directions to develop your angle-creating skills.

- **Positioning:** After creating an angle, position yourself to deliver counterpunches. The angle should provide a clear line of sight to your opponent while minimizing their ability to land effective strikes. Use the angle to your advantage and exploit openings.

2. Tips for Mastery

- **Footwork Drills:** Incorporate footwork drills into your training regimen to enhance your ability to move and create angles effectively. Practice lateral movement, pivoting, and shifting to improve your angle-creating skills.
- **Observation and Adaptation:** Study your opponent's tendencies and adjust your angles based on their movements. Anticipate their attacks and position yourself to exploit their weaknesses. Adapt your angles as the fight progresses to stay ahead of your opponent.
- **Combining Techniques:** Integrate angle creation with other defensive techniques, such as slipping and shoulder rolling. Combining these skills will enhance your overall defensive strategy and make you a more elusive target.

3. Usage and Strategy

- **Avoiding Punches:** Creating angles allows you to avoid punches by positioning yourself outside your opponent's striking range. This strategy is effective for countering opponents who rely on straightforward, linear attacks.
- **Counterattacking:** Use the angles you create to set up counterpunches. By positioning yourself at an advantageous angle, you can exploit openings and

deliver effective strikes while minimizing the risk of being hit.

Clinching and Fighting Inside

Clinching and fighting inside are crucial skills for dealing with opponents who rely on close-range tactics. Clinching involves grabbing and holding your opponent to neutralize their attacks, while fighting inside requires effective techniques to control and land strikes in close quarters.

1. Clinching

Clinching

- **Technique and Execution**
    - **Initiating the Clinch:** To initiate a clinch, close the distance between you and your opponent and use your arms to secure their upper body. Pull them

ADVANCED DEFENSIVE TACTICS

close to neutralize their ability to punch effectively. Keep your arms around their body and use your shoulders to press against them.
- **Control:** Maintain control by keeping your arms wrapped around your opponent's upper body. Use your body weight and leverage to limit their movement and reduce their ability to land effective strikes. Control their head and torso to keep them in a vulnerable position.
- **Breaking the Clinch:** When the referee separates you, use the moment to create distance and resume your offensive strategy. Quick reflexes and awareness of the referee's commands are essential for effective clinching. Be prepared to transition back into an attacking position as soon as the clinch is broken.

2. Fighting Inside

Infighting

- **Technique and Execution**
  - **Close-Range Punching:** Fighting inside involves landing punches from close range. Use short, powerful punches such as hooks and uppercuts to maximize impact in tight spaces. Focus on delivering precise strikes that can penetrate your opponent's defenses.
  - **Body Positioning:** Position yourself close to your opponent to limit their punching range. Use your body to push against them and create openings for your own attacks. Maintain a strong, balanced stance to control the fight in close quarters.
  - **Combining Techniques:** Integrate clinching with close-range punching to control the fight and land effective strikes. Use clinching to neutralize your opponent's attacks and then deliver short, powerful punches when the opportunity arises.

3. Usage and Strategy

- **Neutralizing Opponents:** Use clinching to neutralize opponents who rely on aggressive, close-range tactics. By controlling their movements and reducing their ability to punch, you can gain a strategic advantage. Clinching disrupts their rhythm and limits their offensive capabilities.
  - **Close-Range Advantage:** Fighting inside allows you to capitalize on openings created by clinching and close-range positioning. Use effective punches and body positioning to dominate in close-quarters situations. Take advantage of your proximity to land powerful, close-range strikes.

12

NURTURING A FUTURE OLYMPIC BOXER

RAISING A FUTURE OLYMPIC BOXER IS AN EXCITING and challenging journey that requires commitment, focus, and a strategic approach from both the athlete and their support system. From early engagement to honing advanced skills, creating the right environment for a young boxer to thrive is key. Here are the best practices for guiding a child or young athlete on their path to Olympic boxing success.

1. Early Engagement in Boxing

Start with General Fitness: Before focusing on boxing-specific skills, encourage overall physical fitness with activities like running, jumping, and coordination drills. This builds strength, agility, and endurance that form the foundation for boxing.

Introduce Boxing Basics: Teach the essentials—proper

stance, footwork, and basic punches like the jab, cross, hook, and uppercut. Focus on technique rather than power, as this ensures a solid foundation for future growth.

Balance Fun and Structure: Especially with younger children, keep training fun and engaging. This helps them develop a passion for boxing while improving their skills.

2. Finding the Right Coach and Environment

Qualified Coaching: A skilled coach is crucial to a boxer's development. Look for a coach with experience working with young athletes and a track record of success. They should emphasize safety, technique, and mental toughness.

Positive Gym Culture: Choose a gym that promotes discipline, respect, and hard work. The gym should offer a supportive environment where young boxers can learn, grow, and train safely.

3. Physical Conditioning and Skill Development

Strength and Conditioning: Incorporate exercises to develop explosive power, speed, and endurance. Strength training, cardio, and agility drills are all vital for a boxer's physical development.

Sparring and Practice: Controlled sparring allows young athletes to apply their skills in real-time situations. Focus on defense, movement, and strategy, rather than just brute force.

Regular Competitions: Competing early in local tournaments builds confidence and provides valuable

experience. Over time, these competitions help refine skills and prepare for higher-level challenges.

4. Mental Toughness and Discipline

Building Mental Resilience: Boxing is as much a mental game as a physical one. Encourage young boxers to embrace challenges, learn from mistakes, and stay calm under pressure.

Setting Goals: Help young athletes set short-term and long-term goals to maintain focus. Achievable goals—such as mastering a new technique or winning a local tournament—can keep them motivated and driven.

Visualization: Introduce mental conditioning techniques like visualization. This helps athletes mentally rehearse their performance and prepares them for competition.

5. Nutrition and Recovery

Balanced Diet: A healthy diet is crucial for training and performance. Ensure young boxers consume the right balance of proteins, carbohydrates, and healthy fats to fuel their workouts.

Hydration: Staying hydrated is essential for maintaining energy levels, particularly during long training sessions.

Recovery: Encourage proper recovery with rest days, stretching, and activities like massage to prevent burnout and injury.

6. Parental and Support System Involvement

Encouragement Over Pressure: Parents should provide emotional support and encouragement without creating pressure. Celebrate achievements and help young boxers deal with setbacks constructively.

Providing Resources: Ensure access to the right training equipment, coaching, and competition opportunities. This investment is crucial for skill development.

Emotional Support: Boxing can be mentally and emotionally demanding. Be there for the athlete through wins and losses, offering motivation and understanding.

7. The Road to the Olympics

Commitment: Becoming an Olympic boxer requires long-term commitment and determination. Encourage the athlete to stay focused, even when challenges arise.

Competing at Higher Levels: Participation in national and international competitions is necessary for gaining experience and recognition. These events help young athletes build their profile and work towards the ultimate goal—competing at the Olympics.

13

FILIPINO OLYMPIANS IN BOXING: A LEGACY OF COURAGE AND SKILL

BOXING HAS LONG BEEN ONE OF THE PHILIPPINES' most celebrated sports, producing world-class athletes and a proud legacy on the international stage. For Filipinos, boxing represents more than just a sport—it's a symbol of resilience, strength, and national pride. Filipino boxers have consistently made their mark in the Olympics, standing tall against the best in the world and bringing home medals that solidify their place in the country's sporting history.

The Early Years

The Philippines first competed in the Olympics in 1924, and it wasn't long before Filipino boxers began to show their potential in the sport. In 1932, **Jose Villanueva** became the first Filipino boxer to win an Olympic medal, securing a bronze in the men's bantamweight division at the Los Angeles Games. This achievement marked the Philippines'

Anthony Villanueva

first Olympic medal in boxing and set the stage for future boxers to follow.

Villanueva's success laid the groundwork for Filipino boxing at the Olympics, and in the years that followed, boxing became one of the country's most successful sports in terms of Olympic medal hauls. His son, **Anthony Villanueva**, would later continue the family legacy by winning the country's first silver medal in boxing during the 1964 Tokyo Olympics, where he competed in the featherweight division. This achievement remains a significant milestone in Filipino Olympic history, as it demonstrated the Philippines' growing prowess in boxing.

Leopoldo Serantes: The Resurgence in Seoul

After decades of participation, Filipino boxing saw a resurgence in 1988 when **Leopoldo Serantes** won a bronze medal in the light flyweight division at the Seoul Olympics. His performance reignited national interest in boxing and brought a renewed sense of pride to the sport. Serantes' tenacity and unyielding spirit in the ring epitomized the Filipino fighting heart, making him a national hero and inspiring a new generation of boxers.

Mansueto "Onyok" Velasco: The Unforgettable Silver

Perhaps one of the most famous names in Filipino Olympic boxing is **Mansueto "Onyok" Velasco**, whose journey to the

1996 Atlanta Olympics captivated the nation. Competing in the light flyweight division, Velasco fought his way to the final, where he secured a silver medal, narrowly missing the gold. His impressive run at the Olympics and the controversial decision that awarded the gold to his opponent remain a source of debate among Filipino sports fans.

Mansueto Velasco

Despite the disappointment of not bringing home the gold, Velasco's silver medal was a monumental achievement, solidifying his status as a national icon. Velasco's charisma, humility, and skill in the ring endeared him to Filipinos, and he became a symbol of hope for many aspiring boxers.

The 2020 Tokyo Olympics: A Golden Era for Filipino Boxing

After a long drought in Olympic boxing success, the 2020 Tokyo Olympics proved to be a turning point for the Philippines. With a talented roster of boxers, the country entered the Games with high hopes, and they did not disappoint.

Nesthy Petecio, a trailblazer in women's boxing, won a silver medal in the featherweight division. Petecio's achievement was historic, as she became the first Filipino woman to win an Olympic boxing medal. Her

Nesthy Petecio

emotional journey to the podium was a testament to her hard work, perseverance, and dedication to the sport. Petecio's success has inspired many young girls in the Philippines to pursue boxing, breaking gender barriers in a sport traditionally dominated by men.

In the men's division, **Carlo Paalam** added to the country's medal tally with a silver in the flyweight division.

Carlo Paalam

Paalam's rise to Olympic success was nothing short of remarkable. Coming from humble beginnings, Paalam's story resonates with many Filipinos, as he overcame immense challenges to become one of the best boxers in the world. His performance in Tokyo was a masterclass in skill, determination, and heart, showcasing the true spirit of Filipino boxing.

Eumir Marcial, another standout in Tokyo, secured a bronze medal in the middleweight division. Known for his power and aggression in the ring, Marcial's Olympic run was filled with excitement and drama. His bronze medal was a significant achievement, as it continued the Philippines' rich history in boxing while also setting the stage for Marcial's promising future, both as an amateur and potentially as a professional.

The victories of boxers like Petecio, Paalam, and Marcial in the 2020 Tokyo Olympics have reignited the country's passion for the sport, inspiring the next generation of Filipino athletes to dream of Olympic glory. Their accomplishments also highlight the importance of government and private sector support in nurturing and developing the country's

Eumir Marcial

sports programs. With continued investment in training, facilities, and coaching, the Philippines has the potential to produce even more world-class boxers who can compete at the highest levels.

The Future of Filipino Boxing in the Olympics

The Philippines' long history of boxing excellence, from Jose Villanueva's bronze in 1932 to the multiple medals won in Tokyo 2020, reflects the nation's enduring love for the sport. As new talents emerge and the country's boxing programs continue to improve, Filipino boxers will undoubtedly keep the Olympic dream alive, punching their way to the top of the podium and making their country proud.

LIST OF OLYMPIC MEDALISTS (2000–2024)

Men's Flyweight

Games	Gold	Silver	Bronze
2000 Sydney	Wijan Ponlid Thailand	Bulat Jumadilov Kazakhstan	Wladimir Sidorenko Ukraine Jérôme Thomas France
2004 Athens	Yuriorkis Gamboa Cuba	Jérôme Thomas France	Fuad Aslanov Azerbaijan Rustamhodza Rahimov Germany
2008 Beijing	Somjit Jongjohor Thailand	Andry Laffita Cuba	Vincenzo Picardi Italy Georgy Balakshin Russia
2012 London	Robeisy Ramírez Cuba	Nyambayaryn Tögstsogt Mongolia	Misha Aloyan Russia Michael Conlan Ireland

LIST OF OLYMPIC MEDALISTS (2000–2024)

2016 Rio de Janeiro	Shakhobidin Zoirov Uzbekistan	-	Yoel Finol Venezuela Hu Jianguan China
2020 Tokyo	Galal Yafai Great Britain	Carlo Paalam Philippines	Ryomei Tanaka Japan Saken Bibossinov Kazakhstan
2024 Paris	Hasanboy Dusmatov Uzbekistan	Billal Bennama France	Junior Alcántara Dominican Republic Daniel Varela de Pina Cape Verde

Men's Featherweight

Games	Gold	Silver	Bronze
2000 Sydney	Bekzat Sattarkhanov Kazakhstan	Ricardo Juarez United States	Kamil Djamaloudinov Russia Tahar Tamsamani Morocco
2004 Athens	Aleksei Tishchenko Russia	Kim Song-Guk North Korea	Jo Seok-Hwan South Korea Vitali Tajbert Germany

Games	Gold	Silver	Bronze
2008 Beijing	Vasyl Lomachenko Ukraine	Khedafi Djelkhir France	Yakup Kılıç Turkey Shahin Imranov Azerbaijan
2012–2016	not included in the Olympic program		
2020 Tokyo	Albert Batyrgaziev ROC	Duke Ragan United States	Samuel Takyi Ghana Lázaro Álvarez Cuba
2024 Paris	Abdumalik Khalokov Uzbekistan	Munarbek Seiitbek Uulu Kyrgyzstan	Charlie Senior Australia Javier Ibáñez Bulgaria

Men's Lightweight

Games	Gold	Silver	Bronze
2000 Sydney	Mario Kindelán Cuba	Andreas Kotelnik Ukraine	Cristián Bejarano Mexico Alexander Maletin Russia
2004 Athens	Mario Kindelán Cuba	Amir Khan Great Britain	Murat Khrachev Russia Serik Yeleuov Kazakhstan
2008 Beijing	Aleksei Tishchenko Russia	Daouda Sow France	Hrachik Javakhyan Armenia Yordenis Ugás Cuba

LIST OF OLYMPIC MEDALISTS (2000–2024)

2012 London	Vasyl Lomachenko Ukraine	Han Soon-Chul South Korea	Evaldas Petrauskas Lithuania Yasniel Toledo Cuba
2016 Rio de Janeiro	Robson Conceição Brazil	Sofiane Oumiha France	Lázaro Álvarez Cuba Dorjnyambuugiin Otgondalai Mongolia
2020 Tokyo	Andy Cruz Cuba	Keyshawn Davis United States	Hovhannes Bachkov Armenia Harry Garside Australia
2024 Paris	Erislandy Álvarez Cuba	Sofiane Oumiha France	Wyatt Sanford Canada Lasha Guruli Georgia

Men's Welterweight

Games	Gold	Silver	Bronze
2000 Sydney	Oleg Saitov Russia	Sergey Dotsenko Ukraine	Vitalie Grușac Moldova Dorel Simion Romania
2004 Athens	Bakhtiyar Artayev Kazakhstan	Lorenzo Aragón Cuba	Kim Jung-Joo South Korea

LIST OF OLYMPIC MEDALISTS (2000–2024)

Games	Gold	Silver	Bronze
2008 Beijing	Bakhyt Sarsekbayev Kazakhstan	Carlos Banteaux Cuba	Oleg Saitov Russia Hanati Silamu China Kim Jung-Joo South Korea
2012 London	Serik Sapiyev Kazakhstan	Fred Evans Great Britain	Taras Shelestyuk Ukraine Andrey Zamkovoy Russia
2016 Rio de Janeiro	Daniyar Yeleussinov Kazakhstan	Shakhram Giyasov Uzbekistan	Mohammed Rabii Morocco Souleymane Cissokho France
2020 Tokyo	Roniel Iglesias Cuba	Pat McCormack Great Britain	Aidan Walsh Ireland Andrey Zamkovoy ROC
2024 Paris	Asadkhuja Muydinkhujaev Uzbekistan	Marco Verde Mexico	Omari Jones United States Lewis Richardson Great Britain

Men's Middleweight

Games	Gold	Silver	Bronze
2000 Sydney	Jorge Gutiérrez Cuba	Gaydarbek Gaydarbekov Russia	Vugar Alakbarov Azerbaijan Zsolt Erdei Hungary
2004 Athens	Gaydarbek Gaydarbekov Russia	Gennady Golovkin Kazakhstan	Andre Dirrell United States Prasathinphimai Suriya Thailand
2008 Beijing	James DeGale Great Britain	Emilio Correa Cuba	Darren Sutherland Ireland Vijender Singh India
2012 London	Ryōta Murata Japan	Esquiva Falcão Brazil	Anthony Ogogo Great Britain Abbos Atoev Uzbekistan
2016 Rio de Janeiro	Arlen López Cuba	Bektemir Melikuziev Uzbekistan	Kamran Shakhsuvarly Azerbaijan Misael Rodríguez Mexico
2020 Tokyo	Hebert Conceição Brazil	Oleksandr Khyzhniak Ukraine	Eumir Marcial Philippines Gleb Bakshi ROC

Games	Gold	Silver	Bronze
2024 Paris	Oleksandr Khyzhniak Ukraine	Nurbek Oralbay Kazakhstan	Cristian Pinales Dominican Republic Arlen López Cuba

Men's Heavyweight

Games	Gold	Silver	Bronze
2000 Sydney	Félix Savón Cuba	Sultan Ibragimov Russia	Vladimer Chanturia Georgia Sebastian Köber Germany
2004 Athens	Odlanier Solís Cuba	Viktor Zuyev Belarus	Mohamed Elsayed Egypt Naser Al Shami Syria
2008 Beijing	Rakhim Chakhkiev Russia	Clemente Russo Italy	Osmay Acosta Cuba Deontay Wilder United States
2012 London	Oleksandr Usyk Ukraine	Clemente Russo Italy	Tervel Pulev Bulgaria Teymur Mammadov Azerbaijan

2016 Rio de Janeiro	Evgeny Tishchenko Russia	Vasiliy Levit Kazakhstan	Erislandy Savón Cuba Rustam Tulaganov Uzbekistan
2020 Tokyo	Julio César La Cruz Cuba	Muslim Gadzhimagomedov ROC	David Nyika New Zealand Abner Teixeira Brazil
2024 Paris	Lazizbek Mullojonov Uzbekistan	Loren Alfonso Azerbaijan	Enmanuel Reyes Spain Davlat Boltaev Tajikistan

Men's Super heavyweight

Games	Gold	Silver	Bronze
2000 Sydney	Audley Harrison Great Britain	Mukhtarkhan Dildabekov Kazakhstan	Paolo Vidoz Italy Rustam Saidov Uzbekistan
2004 Athens	Alexander Povetkin Russia	Mohamed Aly Egypt	Michel Lopez Nuñez Cuba Roberto Cammarelle Italy

LIST OF OLYMPIC MEDALISTS (2000–2024)

Games	Gold	Silver	Bronze
2008 Beijing	Roberto Cammarelle, Italy	Zhang Zhilei, China	Vyacheslav Glazkov, Ukraine David Price, Great Britain
2012 London	Anthony Joshua, Great Britain	Roberto Cammarelle, Italy	Ivan Dychko, Kazakhstan Magomedrasul Majidov, Azerbaijan
2016 Rio de Janeiro	Tony Yoka, France	Joe Joyce, Great Britain	Filip Hrgović, Croatia Ivan Dychko, Kazakhstan
2020 Tokyo	Bakhodir Jalolov, Uzbekistan	Richard Torrez, United States	Frazer Clarke, Great Britain Kamshybek Kunkabayev, Kazakhstan
2024 Paris	Bakhodir Jalolov, Uzbekistan	Ayoub Ghadfa, Spain	Nelvie Tiafack, Germany Djamili-Dini Aboudou Moindze, France

LIST OF OLYMPIC MEDALISTS (2000–2024)

Women's Flyweight

Games	Gold	Silver	Bronze
2012 London	Nicola Adams 🇬🇧 Great Britain	Ren Cancan 🇨🇳 China	Marlen Esparza 🇺🇸 United States Mary Kom 🇮🇳 India
2016 Rio de Janeiro	Nicola Adams 🇬🇧 Great Britain	Sarah Ourahmoune 🇫🇷 France	Ren Cancan 🇨🇳 China Ingrit Valencia 🇨🇴 Colombia
2020 Tokyo	Stoyka Krasteva 🇧🇬 Bulgaria	Buse Naz Çakıroğlu 🇹🇷 Turkey	Huang Hsiao-wen Chinese Taipei Tsukimi Namiki 🇯🇵 Japan
2024 Paris	Wu Yu 🇨🇳 China	Buse Naz Çakıroğlu 🇹🇷 Turkey	Nazym Kyzaibay 🇰🇿 Kazakhstan Aira Villegas 🇵🇭 Philippines

Women's Bantamweight

Games	Gold	Silver	Bronze
2024 Paris	Chang Yuan 🇨🇳 China	Hatice Akbaş 🇹🇷 Turkey	Pang Chol-mi 🇰🇵 North Korea Im Ae-ji 🇰🇷 South Korea

LIST OF OLYMPIC MEDALISTS (2000–2024)

Women's Featherweight

Games	Gold	Silver	Bronze
2020 Tokyo	Sena Irie, Japan	Nesthy Petecio, Philippines	Irma Testa, Italy Karriss Artingstall, Great Britain
2024 Paris	Lin Yu-ting, Chinese Taipei	Julia Szeremeta, Poland	Esra Yıldız, Turkey Nesthy Petecio, Philippines

Women's Lightweight

Games	Gold	Silver	Bronze
2012 London	Katie Taylor, Ireland	Sofya Ochigava, Russia	Mavzuna Chorieva, Tajikistan Adriana Araujo, Brazil
2016 Rio de Janeiro	Estelle Mossely, France	Yin Junhua, China	Anastasia Belyakova, Russia Mira Potkonen, Finland
2020 Tokyo	Kellie Harrington, Ireland	Beatriz Ferreira, Brazil	Sudaporn Seesondee, Thailand Mira Potkonen, Finland

LIST OF OLYMPIC MEDALISTS (2000–2024)

| 2024 Paris | Kellie Harrington Ireland | Yang Wenlu China | Wu Shih-yi Chinese Taipei Beatriz Ferreira Brazil |

Women's Welterweight

Games	Gold	Silver	Bronze
2020 Tokyo	Busenaz Sürmeneli Turkey	Gu Hong China	Lovlina Borgohain India Oshae Jones United States
2024 Paris	Imane Khelif Algeria	Yang Liu China	Janjaem Suwannapheng Thailand Chen Nien-chin Chinese Taipei

Women's Middleweight

Games	Gold	Silver	Bronze
2012 London	Claressa Shields United States	Nadezda Torlopova Russia	Marina Volnova Kazakhstan Li Jinzi China

2016 Rio de Janeiro	Claressa Shields 🇺🇸 United States	Nouchka Fontijn 🇳🇱 Netherlands	Dariga Shakimova 🇰🇿 Kazakhstan Li Qian 🇨🇳 China
2020 Tokyo	Lauren Price 🇬🇧 Great Britain	Li Qian 🇨🇳 China	Nouchka Fontijn 🇳🇱 Netherlands Zemfira Magomedalieva 🇷🇺 ROC
2024 Paris	Li Qian 🇨🇳 China	Atheyna Bylon 🇵🇦 Panama	Caitlin Parker 🇦🇺 Australia Cindy Ngamba 🏅 Refugee Olympic Team